Guitar Chord Songbook

Latin Songs

T0079938

ISBN 978-1-4234-6395-5

HAL•LEONARD®
CORPORATION
7777 W. BLUEMOUND RD. P.O. BOX 13819 MILWAUKEE, WI 53213

Visit Hal Leonard Online at
www.halleonard.com

Guitar Chord Songbook

Contents

Adiós

English Words by Eddie Woods
Spanish Translation and Music by Enric Madriguera

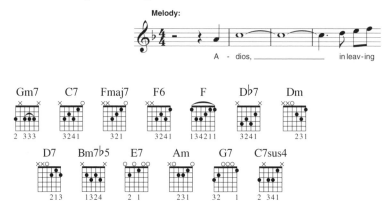

Verse 1

     Gm7 C7 Fmaj7 F6 Gm7 C7
A - diós, _____ in leaving you,

     F   **Gm7 C7 Fmaj7 F6**
It grieves me to say a - diós.

Gm7 C7   **F**
   I'll be so lonely, for you only

 Gm7   **C7**   **F**
I sigh and cry ___ my a - diós,

   D♭7   **C7 Gm7 C7 Fmaj7 F6 Gm7 C7 Fmaj7 F6**
A - diós to you.

Verse 2

     Gm7 C7   **Fmaj7 F6 Gm7 C7**
   And in this heart _____ is mem'ry

       Dm   **D7**
Of what used to be, ___ dear,

   Gm7   **C7**   **F6 Bm7♭5 E7**
For you and me ___ set a - part.

	Am Dm E7

Bridge

Am   Dm   **E7**
Moon watching and waiting a - bove,

Am D7   **G7**   **C7sus4**
Soon it will be bless - ing our love.

Verse 3

C7   Gm7 C7 Fmaj7 F6 Gm7   **C7**
  A - diós, _____ for happy endings

F   **Gm7 C7**
I'll return, dear, to you

D7   **Gm7**   **C7**
With a love true, no more to bid ___ you

   F6 Gm7 C7 Gm7 C7 F6
A - diós.

Translated Lyrics

Verse

Adiós, me voy linda morena lejos de ti
El alma hecha una pena porque al partir
Temo que tu olvides nuestro amor.

Verse

Hermosa flor mi alma cautivaste
Con la fragancia de tu candor.

Bridge

Tu eres toda mi ilusión
Tu eres mi dulce canción.

Verse

Adiós me voy linda morena me voy de aquí
A llorar mi tristeza lejos de ti.

Água de Beber

(Water to Drink)

English Words by Norman Gimbel
Portuguese Words by Vinicius De Moraes
Music by Antonio Carlos Jobim

Melody:

Your love __ is rain, __

Am7 B7#9 E7#5 Fmaj7 Em7b5 B7b9 Dm7 G7 Cmaj7

B7 Bb7b5 A°7 C9/G C7#9/G B7#9/F# E9sus4 D7

Intro

‖: Am7　|B7#9　E7#5　|Am7　　|B7#9　E7#5　|
|Am7　　|Fmaj7　　|Am7　　|Em7b5　　 :‖

Verse 1

```
        Am7              B7b9       E7#5        Am7
        Your love is rain, ___ my heart ___ the flow - er.
                    Dm7      G7          Cmaj7
        I need your love ___ or I ___ will die.
                    B7    Bb7b5  Am7  Ab°7
        My very life ___ is ____ in
                    C9/G  C7#9/G  B7#9/F#
        Your pow - er.
                    B7b9        E9sus4        Am7
        Will I wither and fade or boom to ___ the sky?
```

Chorus 1

```
                    D7  Dm7                 Am7
        Água de beber, _____ give the flower wa - ter to drink.
                    D7  Dm7                     Am7        Em7b5
        Água de beber, _____ give the flower wa - ter to drink.
```

| *Interlude* | \|Am7 | \|B7#9 E7#5 | \|Am7 | \|B7#9 E7#5 | |
| | \|Am7 | \|Fmaj7 | \|Am7 | \| | \| |

Verse 2

                B7#9   **E7#5**   **Am7**
The rain can fall ____ on dis - tant des - erts.

                Dm7   **G7**   **Cmaj7**
The rain can fall ____ upon ____ the sea.

           B7   **Bb7b5 Am7 Ab°7**
The rain can fall ____ up - on

        C9/G C7#9/G B7#9/F#
The flow - er.

      B7b9   **E9sus4**   **Am7**
Since the rain has to fall, let it fall ____ on me.

Chorus 2   *Repeat Chorus 1*

Outro   *Repeat Interlude*

Always in My Heart
(Siempre en Mi Corazón)

Music and Spanish Words by Ernesto Lecuona
English Words by Kim Gannon

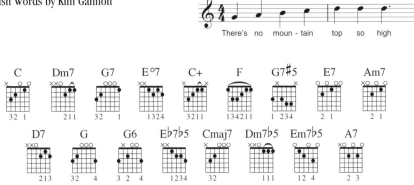

Melody:

There's no moun-tain top so high

C   Dm7   G7   E°7   C+   F   G7#5   E7   Am7

D7   G   G6   Eb7b5   Cmaj7   Dm7b5   Em7b5   A7

Verse

    C   Dm7 G7
There's no mountain top so high

        C   Eb°7   Dm7 G7 C C+
That somehow love can't climb, ____ no, no.

    F   G7   C   Dm7 G7#5
True love will find a way.

    C   Dm7   E7
There's no river quite so wide

      Am7   D7   G G6
That love can't cross in time.

    Am7   Eb7b5   D7 Dm7 G7
Please be - lieve me ____ when I say,

Chorus

N.C.   Cmaj7   G7$\sharp$5   C

You are always in my heart even though you're far a - way.

N.C.   C   E$\flat$°7   Dm7

I can hear the music of the song of love I sang with you.

G7   Dm7   Dm7$\flat$5   G7

You are always in my heart, and when skies a - bove are gray,

          Dm7   G7   E$\flat$°7   C

I remember that you care and then and there the sun breaks through.

N.C.   Cmaj7   G7$\sharp$5   C

Just before I go to sleep there's a rendezvous I keep,

            Em7$\flat$5

And the dreams I always meet

A7   Dm7   Dm7$\flat$5

Help me forget we're far a - part.

N.C.   Dm7$\flat$5

I don't know exactly when, dear,

N.C.   C

But I'm sure we'll meet a - gain, dear,

        E$\flat$°7   G7   C

And, my darling, till we do you are always in my heart.

Translated Lyrics

Chorus   Siempre esta en mi corazón el recuerdo de tu amor,
Que al igual que tu canción quito de mi ama su dolor.
Siempre esta en mi corazón la nostalgia de tu ser
Ya hora puedo comprender que dulce ha sido tu perdón.
La vision de mi sonar me hizo ver con emoción,
Que fue tu alma inspiración donde aplaqué mi sed de amar.
Hoy tan sólo es pero verte y ya nunca más perderte,
Mientras tanto que tu amor, siempre esta en mi corazón.

Amor
(Amor, Amor, Amor)

Music by Gabriel Ruiz
Spanish Words by Ricardo Lopez Mendez
English Words by Norman Newell

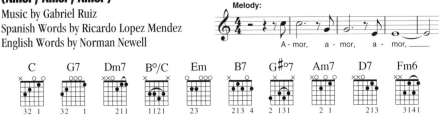

Melody:

A - mor, a - mor, a - mor, _____

C   G7   Dm7   B°/C   Em   B7   G♯°7   Am7   D7   Fm6

Chorus 1

        C
A - mor, amor, amor,

                                  G7
This word so sweet that I repeat means I a - dore you.

Dm7
A - mor, amor, my love,

           G7   **B°/C C**
Would you de - ny this heart that I have placed be - fore   you?

Verse

      Em   **B7**
I can't find another word with meaning so clear,

                        Em
My lips try to whisper sweeter things in your ear.

  G7   **G♯°7**   **Am7**   **D7**
But somehow or other, nothing sounds quite so dear

                G7
As this soft caressing word I know.

Chorus 2

         C
A - mor, amor, my love,

                                     G7
When you're away, there is no day, and nights are lonely.

    Dm7
A - mor, amor, my love,

        G7   **Fm6** **C**
Make love di - vine, say you'll be mine and love me only.

Translated Lyrics

Chorus   Amor, amor, amor nacio de ti,
Nacio de mi de la esperanza.
Amor, amor, amor nacio de Dios,
Para los dos, nacio del alma.

Verse   Sentir que tus besos anidaron en mi,
Igual que palomas mensajeras de luz.
Saber que mis besos se quedaron en ti,
Haciendo en tus labios la senal de la cruz.

Aquellos Ojos Verdes
(Green Eyes)

Music by Nilo Menendez
Spanish Words by Adolfo Utrera
English Words by E. Rivera and E. Woods

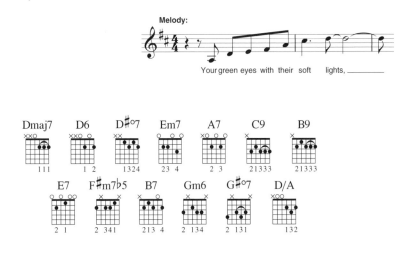

Melody:

Your green eyes with their soft lights, _____

Verse 1

| | N.C. | | | Dmaj7 D6 |
Your green eyes with their soft lights,

Dmaj7
Your eyes that promise sweet nights,

D6 D#°7   Em7
Bring to my soul a longing, _____ a thirst for love di - vine.

A7   Em7   A7   Em7
   In dreams I seem to hold you,   to find you and en - fold you.

A7   C9   B9 E7   A7
   Our lips meet, and our hearts too,   with a thrill so sub - lime.

Verse 2

          Dmaj7 D6
Those cool and limpid green eyes,

                    Dmaj7
A pool where in my love lies ____ so deep,

  F#m7♭5 B7
That in my searching ____ for happiness,

  Em7 B7 Em7
I fear _____ that they will ever haunt me,

Gm6   **G#°7**   **D/A**   **C9**
  All through my life they'll taunt me.

B9   **E7**
  But will they ever want me?

    Em7 A7   **D6**
Green eyes, make my dreams come true.

Translated Lyrics

Verse

Aquellos ojos verdes, de mirada serena.
Dejaron en mi alma eternal sed de amar.
Anbelos de caricias de besos y ternuras
De todas las dulzuras que sabian brindar.

Verse

Aquellos ojos verdes serenos como un lago
En cuyas quietas aguas un dia me miré.
No saben las tristezas que en mi alma han dejado
Aquellos ojos verdes que yo nunca besaré.

Bésame Mucho
(Kiss Me Much)

Music and Spanish Words by Consuelo Velazquez
English Words by Sunny Skylar

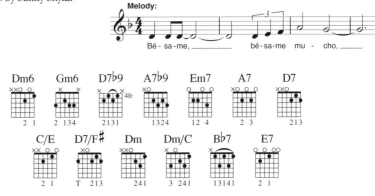

Dm6   Gm6   D7♭9   A7♭9   Em7   A7   D7

C/E   D7/F♯   Dm   Dm/C   B♭7   E7

Verse 1

      Dm6   **Gm6**
Bésame, bésame mucho,

          D7♭9   **Gm6**
Each time I cling to your kiss

       A7♭9   **Dm6 Em7 A7**
I hear music di - vine.

  D7 C/E D7/F♯ **D7♭9 Gm6**
Bé   -   same mucho,

  Dm   **Dm/C**   **B♭7**   **A7**   **Dm6**
Hold me, my darling, and say that you'll always be mine.

Bridge

  Gm6   **Dm6**
This joy is something new, my arms enfolding you,

  A7   **Dm6 D7♭9**
Never knew this thrill be - fore.

  Gm6   **Dm6**
Whoever thought I'd be holding you close to me,

  E7   **B♭7**   **A7**
Whisp'ring, "It's you I a - dore"?

	Dm6			**Gm6**	

Verse 2

| **Dm6** | | **Gm6** |
Dearest one, if you should leave me

| **D7♭9** | **Gm6** |
Each little dream would take wing

| **A7♭9** | **Dm6** | **Em7 A7** |
And my life would be through.

| **D7 C/E D7/F♯ D7♭9 Gm6** |
Be   -   same mucho,

| **Dm** | **Dm/C** | **B♭7** | **A7** | **Dm6** |
Love me for - ever and make all my dreams come true.

Translated Lyrics

Verse
Bésame, bésame mucho,
Como si furra esta noche la última vez.
Bésame mucho,
Que tengo miedo perderte, perderte otra vez.

Bridge
Quiero tenerte muy cerca, mirarme en tus ojos,
Verte junto a mi, piensa que tal vez mañana yo
Ya estare lejos, muy lejos de ti.

Verse
Bésame, bésame mucho,
Como si fuera esta noche la última vez.
Bésame mucho,
Que tengo miedo perderte, perderte despues.

Blame it on the Bossa Nova

Words and Music by
Barry Mann and Cynthia Weil

Melody:

I was at a dance ___

F   C7   B♭

134211   3241   1333

Verse 1

       F   C7
I was at a dance when she caught my eye,

                                F
Standin' all alone, lookin' sad and shy.

                               B♭
We began to dance, swayin' to and fro

   F   C7   F
And soon I knew I'd never let her go.

Chorus 1

                   C7   F
Blame it on the bossa nova with its magic spell.

                   C7   F
Blame it on the bossa nova that she did so well.

             B♭
Oh, it all began with just one little dance,

           F
But soon it ended up a big romance.

              C7   F
Blame it on the bossa nova, the dance of love.

              C7
Now, was it the moon ___ (No, no, the bossa nova!)

          F
Or the stars above? ___ (No, no, the bossa nova!)

           C7
Now, was it the tune? ___ (Yeah, yeah!) The bossa nova!

F   B♭   F
The dance of love.

Verse 2	F C7
	Now that little girl is my bride to be.
	F
	We're gonna raise a family.
	B♭
	And when our kids ask how it came about,
	F C7 F
	I'm gonna say to them without a doubt.
Chorus 2	*Repeat Chorus 1*

Brazil

Original Words and Music by Ary Barroso
English lyrics by S. K. Russell

Melody:

Bra - zil, _____ where hearts were

G6   Am7   D7   Gmaj7   G7   Gb7   F7   E7b9   Cm6   B°7

Verse

        G6   **Am7**
Bra - zil, where hearts were entertaining June,

                       D7
We stood beneath an amber moon

                       G6
And softly murmured, "Someday soon."

    Am7   **D7**   **Gmaj7 G7 Gb7 F7**
We kissed ____ and clung   to - geth - er.

E7b9
Then tomorrow was another day,

The morning found me miles away,

                     Am7
With still a million things to say.

Cm6   **Gmaj7**
Now when twilight dims the sky above,

               Bb°7   **Am7**
Recalling thrills of our ____ love,

D7   **G6**
There's one thing I'm certain of,

    Am7 D7 G6   **Am7 D7**   **G6 (Am7 D7)**
Re - turn ____ I will to old ____ Bra - zil.

Translated Lyrics

Verse

O abre a cortina do passado,
Tira mãe prêta do serrado.
Bota o rei gongo no congã.
¡Brasil! ¡Brasil!
Deixa, cantar de novo o trovador.
Á merencorea luz da lua.
Toda a cancão do meu amor.
Quero ver a "sa dona" caminhando,
Pelos salões arrastando, o seu vestido rendado,
¡Brasil! ¡Brasil! Prá mim prá mim.

Verse

¡Oh, esas palmeras murmurantes,
Donde yo cuelgo mi hamaca,
En noches llenas de splendor!
¡Brasil! ¡Brasil!
¡Oh, en esas fuentes cristalinas
Donde la luna va a mirarse
Domde yo mitigo mi sed!
¡Oh, ese Brasil lindo y moreno,
Es el Brasil brazilero, tierra de samba y canciones!
¡Brasil! ¡Brasil! A mí, a mí.

The Breeze and I

Words by Al Stillman
Music by Ernesto Lecuona

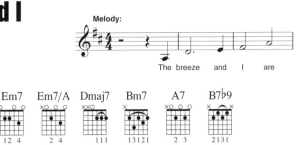

Melody:

The breeze and I are

D6　Cm　Em7　Em7/A　Dmaj7　Bm7　A7　B7♭9

Verse 1

        D6
The breeze and I are saying with a sigh

     Cm   **D6**
That you no longer care.

The breeze and I are whispering goodbye

     Cm   **D6**
To dreams we used to share.

Verse 2

Em7   **Em7/A**   **Dmaj7**   **Bm7**
Ours was a love song that seemed constant as the moon,

            Em7   **A7** **Dmaj7** **B7♭9**
Ending in a strange, mourn - ful tune.

Em7   **Em7/A** **A7** **Dmaj7**
And all a - bout me, they know

         Bm7
You have de - parted without me

       Em7 **A7** **D6**   **A7**   **D6** **(A7)**
And we won - der why, the breeze and I.

GUITAR CHORD SONGBOOK

Chega de Saudade
(No More Blues)

English Lyric by Jon Hendricks and Jessie Cavanaugh
Original Text by Vinicius de Moraes
Music by Antonio Carlos Jobim

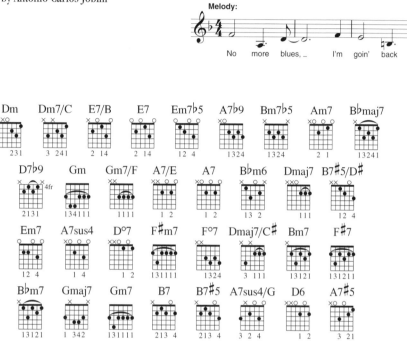

Verse 1

      Dm   **Dm7/C** **E7/B**   **E7**
No more blues, ___ I'm goin' back home.

        Em7♭5   **A7♭9**   **Dm**   **Em7♭5** **A7♭9**
No, no more blues, ___ I prom - ise no more to roam.

Dm   **Bm7♭5** **E7**   **Am7**
Home is where _____ the heart is,

            B♭maj7   **A7♭9**
The funny part ___ is my heart's been right ___ there all along.

Verse 2

Dm   Dm7/C   E7/B   E7
No more tears ____ and no more sighs,

     Em7♭5   A7♭9   Dm
And no more fears, ____ I'll say ____ no more goodbyes.

D7♭9   Gm Gm7/F   A7/E A7
   If travel beck - ons me,

       Dm   Dm7/C
I swear ____ I'm gonna re - fuse.

       Bm7♭5   B♭m6   Dm A7
I'm gonna settle down, and there'll ____ be no more blues.

Verse 3

Dmaj7   B7♯5/D♯   Em7
Ev'ry day ____ while I am far away,

          A7sus4   A7   D°7 Dmaj7
My thoughts turn homeward, ____ forever home - ward.

  F♯m7   F°7   Em7
I travelled 'round the world ____ in search of hap - piness,

       E7   Em7♭5 A7
But all my hap - piness I found was in my home - town.

Verse 4

Dmaj7   Dmaj7/C♯   Bm7   E7
No   more blues, ____ I'm goin' back home.

    F♯7   A7   Bm7   B♭m7   Am7
No, no more dues, ____ I'm through with all my won - derin'.

D7♭9   Gmaj7   Gm7
   Now I'll ____ settle down and live my life

   F♯m7   B7   B7♯5
And build a home and find a wife.

    E7   Em7   A7sus4/G   F♯m7
When we settle down, there'll ____ be no more blues,

     B7♯5
Nothin' but happiness.

    E7   Em7   A7sus4   D6 (A7♯5)
When we settle down, there'll ____ be no more blues.

Translated Lyrics

Verse   Vai minha tristleza e diz a ela,
Que sem ela não pode ser.
Dizlhe numa prece, que ela regresse,
Porque eu não posso mais sofrer.

Verse   Chega de saudade a realidade é que sem ela não há paz
Não há beleza, é só tristeza é a melancholia que não
Sai de mim, não sai de mim, não sai.

Verse   Mas, se ela voltar se ela voltar,
Que coisa linda, que coisa louca.
Pois há menos peixinhos a nadar no mar,
Do que os beijinhos que eu darei na sua boca.

Call Me

Words and Music by Tony Hatch

Verse 1

Cmaj7
If you're feeling sad and lonely,

Cm7   F7
 There's a service I can ren - der.

B♭maj7
 Tell the one who loves you only,

B♭m7   E♭7
 I can be so warm and ten - der.

A♭maj7 Fm7   A♭maj7
Call me! Don't be afraid, you can call me.

Fm7   A♭maj7
Maybe it's late, but just call me.

Fm7   Cmaj7 Dm7 G7
Tell me and I'll be a - round.

Verse 2

Cmaj7
When it seems your friends desert you,

Cm7   F7
 There's somebody thinking of ___ you.

B♭maj7
 I'm the one who'll never hurt you.

B♭m7   E♭7
 Maybe that's because I love you.

A♭maj7 Fm7   A♭maj7
Call me! Don't be afraid, you can call me.

Fm7   A♭maj7
Maybe it's late, but just call me.

Fm7   Cmaj7
Tell me and I'll be a - round.

Em7 A7♭9   Dm7   G7   Dm7 G7
Bridge   Now don't for - get me, ___ 'cause if you let me,

Cmaj7   Em7
I will always stay by you.

A7♭9   Dm7   G7   Dm7 G7
You gotta trust me, ___ that's how it must be.

Cmaj7   Dm7 G7
There's so much that I can do.

Cmaj7
Verse 3   If you call, I'll be right with you.

Cm7   F7
You and I should be togeth - er.

B♭maj7
Take this love I long to give you,

B♭m7   E♭7
I'll be at your side for - ever.

A♭maj7 Fm7   A♭maj7
Call me! Don't be afraid, you can call me.

Fm7   A♭maj7
Maybe it's late, but just call me.

Fm7   Cmaj7 (Dm7 G7)
Tell me and I'll be a - round.

The Constant Rain
(Chove Chuva)

Original Words and Music by Jorge Ben
English Words by Norman Gimbel

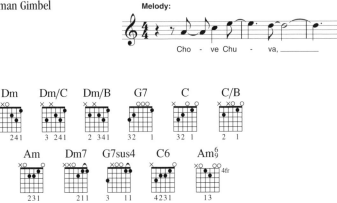

Verse

        N.C.   **Dm Dm/C Dm/B**   **G7**   **C C/B**
Chove Chu - va, _____ con - stant is the rain.

        Am   **Dm Dm/C Dm/B**   **G7**   **C C/B**
Chove Chu - va, _____end - less is a pain.

        Am   **Dm7**
As I stand here and re - member

        G7sus4 **G7**   **C**
That once our ___ hearts were one,

                   Dm7
And ev'ry day was spring to me

              G7   **C6**
Till you left and took away the sun.

               Dm7   **G7**   **Dm7**
Now the days are lonely, the song of love is still.

        G7   **Dm7**   **G7**   **C**
They say that I'll for - get you but I say I never will.

                              Dm7   **G7sus4**
And it hurts with such a pain to be a - lone,

        G7   **C6**
And lonely in the rain.

Am   **Dm7**   **G7**
    And it hurts with such a pain to be a - lone,

                      C
And lonely in the rain.

Am   **Dm Dm/C Dm/B**
    Chove Chu - va,

        G7   **C C/B**
Con - stant is the rain.

Am   **Dm Dm/C Dm/B**
    Chove Chu - va,

        G7   **C   Am⁶**
End - less is the pain.

Translated Lyrics

                    Chove Chuva, chove sem parar.
                    Chove Chuva, chove sem parar.
                    Pois eu fazer uma prece
                    Pra dues nossos Senhor Pra chuva parar
                    De mo lhar o meu divino amor
                    Que é muito lindo é mais que o infi
                    Nito é puro é beloinocente como a flor.
                    Por favor chuva ruim
                    Nao molhe mais o meu amor assim.
                    Por favor chuva ruim
                    Nao molhe mais o meu amor assim.
                    Chove Chuva, chove sem parar.
                    Chove Chuva, chove sem parar.

A Day in the Life of a Fool
(Manhã de Carnaval)

Words by Carl Sigman
Music by Luiz Bonfa

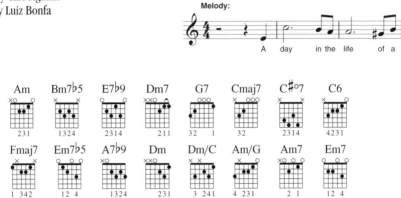

Melody:

A day   in the   life   of a

Am   Bm7♭5   E7♭9   Dm7   G7   Cmaj7   C#°7   C6

Fmaj7   Em7♭5   A7♭9   Dm   Dm/C   Am/G   Am7   Em7

Verse 1

    Am   Bm7♭5 E7♭9 Am Bm7♭5 E7♭9
A day in the life   of a   fool,

    Am   Dm7 G7   Cmaj7
A sad and a long, ____ lonely day.

C#°7   Dm7   G7   C6   Fmaj7
  I walk the avenue ____ and hope I'll run into

         Bm7♭5   E7♭9   Am Bm7♭5 E7♭9
The welcome sight of you ____ coming my way.

Verse 2

    Am   **Bm7♭5** **E7♭9**   **Am Bm7♭5 E7♭9**
I stop just a - cross _____ from your door,

      Em7♭5   **A7♭9**   **Dm**
But you're never home any more.

        Dm/C   **Bm7♭5** **E7♭9**
So back _____ to my room

 Am   **Am/G**   **Fmaj7 Bm7♭5**
 And there in the gloom I cry

E7♭9   **Am Bm7♭5 E7♭9**
 Tears of good - bye.

 Am   **Dm7**   **Am7**   **Dm7**   **Am7**
 Till you come back to me, that's the way it will be

     Dm7   **Em7**   **Am**
Ev'ry day in the life of a fool.

Dindi

Music by Antonio Carlos Jobim
Portuguese Lyrics by Aloysio de Oliveira
English Lyrics by Ray Gilbert

Melody:

Sky,   so vast in the   sky   with far - a - way

Dmaj7   Cmaj7   Bmaj7   G#m7   C#m9   F#13   Am7   D7   Gmaj7   C9b5

D6   G#m7b5   C#7   F#m   Dm6   B7b9   Em   Cm6   Em7   A7

Verse

Dmaj7   Cmaj7   Dmaj7   Cmaj7
Sky, so vast in the sky with faraway clouds just wondering by.

Bmaj7   G#m7   C#m9   F#13
Where do they go? ___ Oh, I don't know, don't know.

Dmaj7   Cmaj7   Dmaj7   Cmaj7
Wind that speaks to the leaves telling stories that no one be - lieves,

Bmaj7   G#m7   C#m9   F#13
Stories of love ___ belong to you and me.

Chorus

Dmaj7   Cmaj7   Dmaj7
Oh, Dindi, ___ if I only had words

        Am7   D7   Gmaj7
I would say all the beautiful things that I see

C9b5   D6   Am7
When you're with me. Oh, my Dindi.

Dmaj7   Cmaj7   Dmaj7   Am7
Oh, Dindi, ___ like the song of the wind in the trees,

        D7   Gmaj7
That's how my heart is singing, Dindi,

C9b5   D6   G#m7b5 C#7
Happy, Dindi, when you're with me.

Bridge

F#m   Dm6
I love you more each day,

    F#m Dm6   F#m B7b9
Yes, I do, _____ yes, I do.

Em   Cm6
I'd let you go a - way

    Em Cm6   Em7
If you take _____ me with you.

Outro

A7   Dmaj7   Cmaj7   Dmaj7
Don't you know, Dindi, ____ I'd be running and searching

   Am7   D7   Gmaj7
For you like a river that can't find the sea,

C9b5   D6   (Am7)
That would be me without you, my Dindi.

Translated Lyrics

Verse

Ceu tâo grandee o ceu e bandos
De nuvens que passam ligeiras.
Aonde elas vâo, Ah, eu nâo sei, nao sei.
Eo vento que fala nas folhas contando
As historias que sâo de ninguem,
Mas que sâo minhas e de voce tambem.

Chorus

Ah, Dindi se soubesses o bem que te quero
O mundo seria Dindi lindo Dindi tudo Dindi.
Ah, Dindi se um dia voce for embora nie
Lava contigo Dindi fica, Dindi, Olha Dindi.

Bridge

E as aguas deste rio
Onde vâo, eu nao sei,
A minha vida inteira, esperei, esperei

Outro

Por voce Dindi
Que é a coisa mais linda que
Existe voce nao existe Dindi
Deixa Dindi que eu te adore Dindi.

Estate

Music by Bruno Martino
Lyrics by Bruno Brighetti

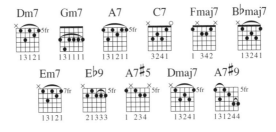

Verse 1

      Dm7   **Gm7**   **A7**   **Dm7**
E - state sei calda come i baci che ho per - duto

     Gm7   **C7**   **Fmaj7**
Sei picna di un a - more che è pas - sato

      B♭maj7   **Gm7**   **Em7**
Che il cuore mio vor - rabbe cancel - lar.

Verse 2

    A7 **E♭9**   **Dm7**
    Odio l' e - state.

   Gm7   **A7**   **Dm7**
Il sole che ogni giorno ci scal - dava,

   Gm7   **C7**   **Fmaj7**
Che splendid tra - monti dipin - geva

    B♭maj7   **Gm7**   **Em7**
A - dresso brunia solo confu - ror.

Bridge

A7   A7#5   Dmaj7
Torne - rá un altro in - verno,

Em7   A7   Dmaj7
Ca - dranno mille petali di rose

Gm7   C7   Fmaj7
La neve copri - rà tutte le cose

Bbmaj7   Gm7   Em7
E forse po' di pace torne - rà.

Verse 3

A7 Eb9   Dm7
Odio l' e - state.

Gm7   A7   Dm7
Che ha dato il suo pro - fumo ad ogni fiore,

Gm7   C7   Fmaj7
L' e - state che ha creato il nosstro a - more

Bbmaj7   Gm7   Em7
Per farmi poi mor - riro di do - lor.

A7 Eb9   Dm7 Gm7 A7#9   Dm7
Odio l' e - state. _____ Odio l'a - state.

A Felicidade

Words and Music by Vinicius de Moraes
and Antonio Carlos Jobim

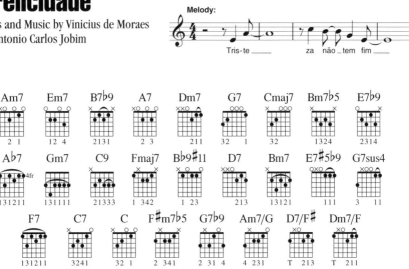

Verse 1

      Am7
Triste ____ za não tem fim.

    Em7 B7♭9 Em7 A7 Dm7 G7
Feli - cida - de sim.

Cmaj7 Bm7♭5   **E7♭9**
A felicida - de é como a go - ta.

     Am7   **A♭7**   **Gm7 C9**
De orval - ha numa pe - ta la de flor.

Fmaj7   **B♭9♯11**   **Am7**   **D7**
  Brilha tranquil - la depois ____ de leve oscil - la.

   Am7   **Bm7** **E7♯5♭9**   **Am7 G7sus4 G7**
E cai ____ como una la - grima ____ de amor.

Verse 2

Cmaj7   F7   Cmaj7
A felicida - de do pobre pa - rece.

  Gm7   C7   Fmaj7
A ___ grande i lu são ___ do carnaval.

  Dm7   G7   C
A gente trabal - ha o aho en teiro.

  F#m7b5   B7b9
Por un momento de - sonho.

    Em7   A7   Dm7 G7b9
Prafa - zer a fan - tas - ia.

    Am7   Am7/G   D7/F#
De rei ___ ou de pira - ta ou jardinei - ra.

Dm7/F Am7   Bm7b5   E7#5b9 Am7
E tu   -   do se acaber ___ na quar - ta fei - ra.

Verse 3

     Am7
Triste ___ za não tem fim.

  Em7 B7b9   Em7 A7 Dm7 G7
Feli - cida - de sim.

Cmaj7 Bm7b5   E7b9
A felicida - de é como a plu - ma.

       Am7   Ab7   Gm7 C9
Que o ventu - vae levan - do peloar.

Fmaj7   Bb9#11   Am7 D7
  Voa tao leve mas ___ tem la vida bre - ve.

  Am7   Bm7   E7#5b9 Am7
Preci - sa que haja vento sem - parar.

        Bm7   E7#5b9 Am7
Precisa que haja vento sem - parar.

        Bm7   E7#5b9 Am7
Precisa que haja vento sem - parar.

    F#maj7b5 Am7
Triste za não tem fim.

Frensí

English Words by Leonard Whitcup
Original Spanish version by Alberto Dominguez

Melody:

Some-time a - go I wan-dered down in - to

C   Dm7   G7   E   F#m7   B7

C6   Dm6   Emaj7   Am7   D7

Verse

     C   Dm7   G7   C   Dm7 G7
Sometime ago   I wandered down into old Mexico.

     C   Dm7   G7   C
While I was there   I felt ro - mance ev'ry - where.

     E
Moon was shining bright

     F#m7   B7   E   F#m7 B7
And I could hear laughing voices in the night.

     E   F#m7   B7   E   G7
Ev'ryone was gay,   this was the start of their holi - day.

Chorus

     N.C.   Dm7 G7
It was Fiesta down in Mexi - co,

Dm7   G7   Dm7   G7
    And so I stopped awhile to see the show.

Dm7   G7   C6
    I knew that frenesi meant "Please love me"

Dm6   G7   C6
    And I could say "Frene - sí."

N.C.   Dm7   G7
A lovely señorita caught my eye.

```
Dm7          G7              Dm7      G7
   I stood en - chanted as she wandered by,

Dm7       G7            C6
   And never knowing that it came from me

Dm6      G7           C6
   I gently sighed, "Frene - sí."

N.C.                                    Emaj7
She stopped and raised her eyes to mine,

Dm6                      Emaj7
   Her lips just pleaded to be kissed.

N.C.                             Emaj7
Her eyes were soft as candle - shine,

Am7          D7       Dm7 G7
   So how was I to re - sist?

     N.C.                    Dm7    G7
And now without a heart to call my own,

Dm7        G7           Dm7  G7
   A greater happiness I've never  known

Dm7          G7           C6
   Because her kisses are for me alone,

Dm7              G7          C6
   Who wouldn't say "Frene - sí."
```

Translated Lyrics

Verse

Bésame tú a mí, bésame igual que mi boca te beso,
Dame el frenesí que mi locura te dío.
¿Quien, si no fuí yo, pudo enseñarte el camino del amor,
Muerta mi altivez, cuando mi orgullo rodó a tus pies?

Chorus

Quiero que vivas sòlo para mí y que tú vayas por donde yo voy,
Para que mi alma sea no más de ti, bésame con frenesí.
Dama la luz que tiene tu mirar y la ansiedad que entre tus labios vi,
Esa locura de vivir y amar, que es más que amor, frenesí.
Hay en el beso que te dí, alma, piedad, corazón,
Dime que sabes tu sentir, lo mismo que siento yo.
Quiero que vivas sòlo para mí y que tú vayas pordonde yo voy,
Para que mi alma sea no más de tí, bésame con frenesí.

The Gift!
(Recado Bossa Nova)

Music by Djalma Ferreira
Original Lyric by Luiz Antonio
English Lyric by Paul Francis Webster

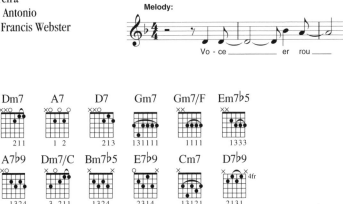

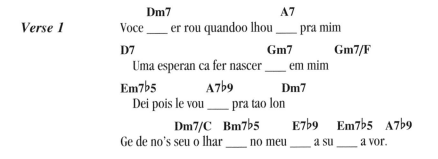

Verse 1

   Dm7   **A7**
Voce ___ er rou quandoo lhou ___ pra mim

D7   **Gm7**   **Gm7/F**
 Uma esperan ca fer nascer ___ em mim

Em7♭5   **A7♭9**   **Dm7**
 Dei pois le vou ___ pra tao lon

    Dm7/C **Bm7♭5**   **E7♭9** **Em7♭5** **A7♭9**
Ge de no's seu o lhar ___ no meu ___ a su ___ a vor.

	Dm7	A7
Verse 2	Voce ___ dei xou semquerer ___ dei xou	

Verse 2

        Dm7   A7
Verse 2   Voce ___ dei xou semquerer ___ dei xou

        D7   Gm7   Gm7/F
        Uma saudade e nor me em seu ___ lugar

        Em7♭5   A7♭9   Dm7
          De pois no's dois ___ cada qual

                       Cm7   A7♭9   Dm7
        A mer ce do seu desti ___ no voce seu mim eu sem vo - ce.

        D7♭9   Gm7
Bridge   Sau - dade me uma beque de reca - do

        E7♭9   Am7 A7♭9
        Nao diga que eu me encon tro nêsse es ta - do.

Verse 3   *Repeat Verse 1*

The Girl from Ipanema
(Garôta de Ipanema)

Music by Antonio Carlos Jobim
English Words by Norman Gimbel
Original Words by Vinicius de Moraes

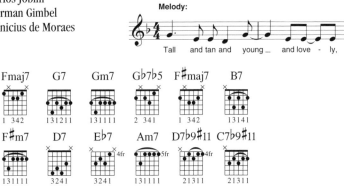

Melody:

Tall and tan and young _ and love - ly,

Verse 1

      Fmaj7
Tall and tan and young and lovely,

        G7
The girl ____ from Ipanema goes walking,

        Gm7
And when ____ she passes,

        G♭7♭5   **Fmaj7 G♭7♭5**
Each one ____ she passes goes   "Ah!"

Verse 2

      Fmaj7
When she walks she's like a samba

        G7
That swings ____ so cool and sways so gentle,

        Gm7
That when ____ she passes,

        G♭7♭5   **Fmaj7**
Each one ____ she passes goes   "Ah!"

Bridge

F#maj7   B7
Oh, but I watch her so sadly.

    F#m7   D7
How ___ can I tell her I love her?

    Gm7   E♭7
Yes, ___ I would give my heart gladly,

        Am7   D7♭9#11
But each day when she walks to the sea

    Gm7   C7♭9#11
She looks straight ahead not at me.

Verse 3

Fmaj7
Tall and tan and young and lovely,

    G7
The girl ___ from Ipanema goes walking,

    Gm7
And when ___ she passes,

   G♭7♭5   Fmaj7
I smile, ___ but she doesn't see.

G♭7♭5   Fmaj7
  She just doesn't see.

G♭7♭5   Fmaj7
  No, she doesn't see.

Granada

Spanish Words and Music by Agustin Lara
English Words by Dorothy Dodd

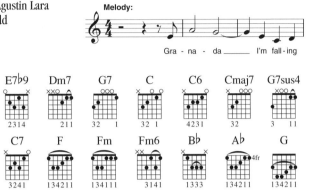

Melody:

Gra - na - da _____ I'm fall-ing

Am   E   F   E7♭9   Dm7   G7   C   C6   Cmaj7   G7sus4

Em   B7   C#°7   C7   F   Fm   Fm6   B♭   A♭   G

Intro

                    Am
Gra - nada, I'm falling under your spell,

And if you could speak what a fascinating tale you would tell
        E   F   E
Of an age the world has long for - gotten,
                        F   E7♭9 Dm7
Of an age that weaves a silent magic in Granada to - day.

Verse 1

        G7 N.C. C   C6   Cmaj7   C   G7
              The dawn in the sky greets the day with a sigh for Gra - nada.
            G7sus4   G7   Dm7   G7   C6
For she can re - member the splendor that once was __ Gra - nada.
        C   C6   Cmaj7   C
It still can be found in the hills all a - round
        Em   B7   Em
As I wander along en - tranced by the beauty be - fore,
        B7   Em   C#°7 G7
Entranced by a land full of sunshine and flow - ers and song.

              C   **C6**   **Cmaj7**   **C**   **G7**

Verse 2   And when day is done and the sun starts to set in Gra - nada,

              G7sus4   **G7**   **Dm7 G7**   **C6**

        I envy the blush of the snowclad Si - erra _____ Ne - vada.

C   **C7**   **F**

        For soon it will welcome the stars

        Fm   **C**   **Fm6**   **C**

While a thousand gui - tars play a soft haban - era.

        Fm   **C**   **G7**

Then moonlit Granada will live again the glory of yesterday,

              C Bb Ab G C

Romantic and gay.

How Insensitive
(Insensatez)

Music by Antonio Carlos Jobim
Original Words by Vinicius de Moraes
English Words by Norman Gimbel

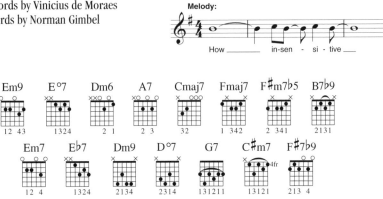

Melody:

How _____ in-sen - si - tive _____

Verse 1

| Em9   Eb°7   Dm6 |
| How insensitive ____ I must have seemed |

| A7 |
| When she told me that she loved ____ me. |

| Cmaj7   Fmaj7   F#m7b5 |
| How unmoved and cold ____ I must have seemed |

| B7b9   Em7 Eb7 |
| When she told me so sincere - ly. |

Verse 2

| Dm9   Db°7   Cmaj7 |
| Why, she must have asked, ____ did I just turn |

| F#m7b5 B7b9 Em7   Eb7 |
| And stare in   icy si - lence? |

| Dm9 G7   C#m7 |
| What ____ was I to say? |

| F#7b9   Cmaj7   B7b9   Em7 F#m7b5 B7b9 |
| What do you say ____ when a love affair is o - ver? |

Verse 3

Em9   Eb°7   Dm6
Now she's gone away ___ and I'm a - lone

           A7
With the mem'ry of her last ___ look.

Cmaj7   Fmaj7 F#m7b5
Vague, drawn and sad, ___ I see it still,

  B7b9   Em7 Eb7
All her heartbreak in that last ___ look.

Verse 4

Dm9   Db°7   Cmaj7
How, she must have asked, ___ could I just turn

  F#m7b5 B7b9 Em7 Eb7
And stare in icy si - lence?

Dm9 G7   C#m7
What ___ was I to do?

F#7b9   Cmaj7 B7b9   Em7
 What do you do ___ when a love affair is o - ver?

It's Impossible

(Somos Novios)

English Lyric by Sid Wayne
Spanish Words and Music by Armando Manzanero

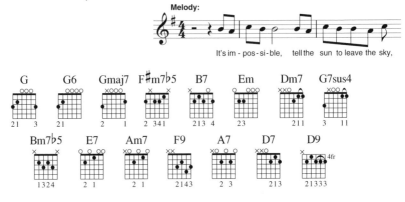

Verse 1

           G   **G6**   **Gmaj7**   **G6**
It's im - possible, ___ tell the sun to leave the sky,

        F#m7♭5
It's just im - possible.

B7   **Em**   **Dm7**   **G7sus4**
  It's im - possible, ask a baby not to cry,

       Bm7♭5
It's just im - possible.

E7   **Am7**   **F9**
  Can I hold you closer to me,

      Gmaj7   **E7**
And not feel you going through me?

      Am7   **A7**
Split the second that I never think of you?

      D7
Oh, how im - possible.

| | | Am7 D7 | G | G6 | | Gmaj7 | G6 |
Verse 2

Am7 D7   G   G6   Gmaj7   G6

Verse 2   Can the ocean ____ keep from rushing to the shore?

F#m7b5

It's just im - possible.

B7   Em   Dm7   G7sus4

If I had you, could I ever want for more?

Bm7b5

It's just im - possible.

E7   Am7   F9

And to - morrow, should you ask me for the world,

G7sus4

Somehow I'd get it.

E7   Am7

I would sell my very soul and not re - gret it,

D9   G6   (Am7 D7)

For to live without your love is just im - possible.

Translated Lyrics

Verse 1   Somos novios pues los dos sentimos mu tuo amor profundo
Y con eso ya ganamos lo más grande de este mundo.
Nos amamos nos besamos como novios nos deseamos
Y hasta a veces sin sotivo sin razón nos enojamos.

Verse 2   Somos novios mantenemos un caerno limpio y puro.
Como todos procuramos el momento más oscuro
Para hablarnos para darnos el más dulce de los besos
Recordar de que color son los cerezos
Sin hacer más comentarios somos novios.

Kiss of Fire

Words and Music by
Lester Allen and Robert Hill
(Adapted from A.G. Villoldo)

I touch your lips and all at once the sparks go

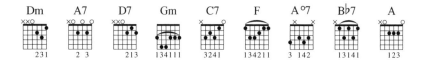

Verse 1

          Dm
I touch your lips and all at once the sparks go flying.

                       A7
Those devil lips that know so well the art of lying.

And tho' I see the danger, still the flame grows higher.

                     Dm
I know I must surrender to your kiss of fire.

Verse 2

          Dm
Just like a torch, you set the soul within me burning.

          D7   **Gm**
I must go on along this road of no re - turning.

                    Dm
And tho' it burns me and it turns me into ashes,

          A7   **Dm**
My whole world crashes without your kiss of fire.

Bridge

             C7   **F**
I can't re - sist you, what good is there in trying?

            A♭°7   **C7**   **F**
What good is there de - nying you're all that I de - sire?

         A7   **Dm**
Since first I kissed you, my heart was yours com - pletely.

       B♭7   **A**
If I'm a slave, then it's a slave I want to be.

      B♭7 **A7**   **B♭7** **A7**
Don't pity   me, don't pity   me.

Verse 3

          Dm
Give me your lips, the lips you only let me borrow.

         D7   **Gm**
Love me to - night and let the devil take to - morrow.

                      Dm
I know that I must have your kiss although it dooms me,

       A7   **Dm**
Tho' it con - sumes me, your kiss of fire.

Little Boat

Original Lyric by Ronaldo Boscoli
English Lyric by Buddy Kaye
Music by Roberto Menescal

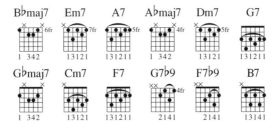

Verse 1

B♭maj7   Em7 A7
My little boat is like a note bouncing merrily a - long,

  Em7   A7
Hear it splashing up a song.

A♭maj7
The sails are white, the sky is bright

  Dm7   G7   Dm7 G7
Heading out into the blue with a crew of only two,

G♭maj7
Where we can share love's salty air

  Cm7 F7   Cm7
On a little para - dise that's a - float.

F7 Dm7 G7♭9 Cm7 F7♭9
Not a care have we in my little boat.

                   B♭maj7   **Em7**   **A7**
Verse 2   The wind is still, we feel the thrill of a voyage heaven bound,

                          Em7   **A7**
                   Though we only drift a - round,

                   A♭maj7
                   Warmed by the sun, two hearts as one

                          Dm7   **G7**   **Dm7**   **G7**
                   Beating with enchanted bliss, melting in each other's kiss.

                   G♭maj7
                   When daylight ends and slyly sends

                         Cm7   **F7**   **Cm7**
                   Little stars to twilight brightly a - bove,

                   F7   **Dm7 G7♭9   Cm7   F7♭9**
                     It's good - bye to my little boat of love.

                   B♭maj7 B7   B♭maj7
Outro   ‖: Good - bye, little boat.   :‖

The Look of Love
from CASINO ROYALE

Words by Hal David
Music by Burt Bacharach

Melody:

The look ___ of love ___

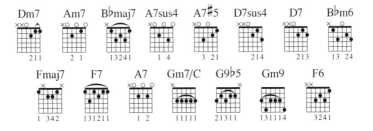

Dm7 Am7 B♭maj7 A7sus4 A7#5 D7sus4 D7 B♭m6

Fmaj7 F7 A7 Gm7/C G9♭5 Gm9 F6

Verse 1

       Dm7   **Am7**
The look ___ of love is in ___ your eyes,

       B♭maj7   **A7sus4**
A look ___ your smile can't disguise.

A7#5   **Dm7**   **D7sus4 D7**
  The look ___ of love

B♭maj7   **B♭m6**
  Is saying so ___ much more

                           Fmaj7 F7
Than just words could ever say.

B♭maj7   **A7sus4**   **A7**
  And what my heart has heard, well, it takes my breath a - way.

Gm7/C   **Fmaj7**   **Gm7/C**
  I can hard - ly wait to hold you, feel ___ my arms around you,

Fmaj7   **Gm7/C Fmaj7**
  How long I have waited,   waited just to love you.

Verse 2

Gm7/C   A7#5   Dm7
Now ___ that I have found you, you've got the look ___ of love,

   Am7   B♭maj7   A7sus4
It's on ___ your face, a look ___ that time can't erase.

A7#5   Dm7   D7sus4 D7
Be mine ___ tonight,

B♭maj7   B♭m6
Let this be just ___ the start

                Fmaj7 F7
Of so many nights like this.

B♭maj7   A7sus4   A7
Let's take a lover's vow and then seal it with a kiss.

Gm7/C   Fmaj7   Gm7/C
I can hard - ly wait to hold you, feel ___ my arms around you,

Fmaj7   Gm7/C Fmaj7
How long I have waited,   waited just to love you.

   Gm7/C   A7#5   Dm7   G9♭5
Now ___ that I have found you don't ever go, don't ever go.

Gm9 Gm7/C   F6
I love you so.

Love Me with All Your Heart
(Cuando Caliente el Sol)

Original Words and Music by
Carlos Rigual and Carlos A. Martinoli
English Words by Sunny Skylar

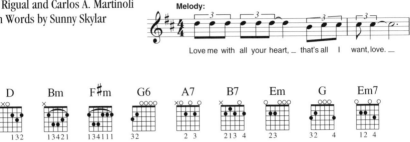

Love me with all your heart, __ that's all I want, love. __

D   Bm   F#m   G6   A7   B7   Em   G   Em7

Verse 1

            D   Bm   F#m
Love me with all your heart, ____ that's all I want, love.

G6   A7   D B7
Love me with all of your heart or not at all.

Em   A7   D   Bm
Just promise me this, that you'll give me all your kisses,

         F#m   G   A7
Ev'ry winter, ev'ry summer, ev'ry fall.

Verse 2

            D   Bm   F#m
When we are far apart ____ or when you're near me,

G6   A7   D B7
Love me with all of your heart as I love you.

Em   A7   D   Bm
Don't give me your love for a moment or an hour,

         F#m   G   A7
Love me always as you loved me from the start,

                          D Bm Em7 A7 D
With ev'ry beat of your heart.

Translated Lyrics

Verse 1
Cuando calienta el sol aquí en la playa
Siento tu cuerpo vibrar cerca de mí,
Es tu palpitar es tu cara es tu pelo
Son tus besos me estremezco.

Verse 2
Cuando caliente el sol aquí en la playa,
Siento tu cuerpo vibrar cerca de mí,
Es tu palpitar tu recuerdo mi locura
Mi delirio me estremezco,
Cuando calienta el sol.

Mambo Jambo
(Que Rico el Mambo)

English Words by Raymond Karl and Charlie Towne
Original Words and Music by Damaso Perez Prado

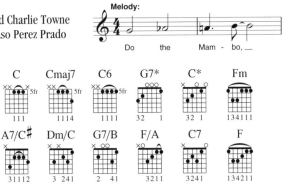

Melody:

Do   the   Mam - bo, ___

G7   G7♭9   G9   C   Cmaj7   C6   G7*   C*   Fm

F6   A   Dm   A7/C♯   Dm/C   G7/B   F/A   C7   F

Chorus 1

|:
G7 G7♭9 G9   G7
Do   the   Mam - bo,

G7 G7♭9 G9   G7
Do   the   Mam - bo,

C   Cmaj7 C6   C
Mam - bo   Jam - bo,

      Cmaj7 C6   C
Mam - bo   Jam - bo. :||

Verse 1

G7   G7♭9   G9   G7
Do it with someone you madly a - dore,

         G7♭9   G9   G7
Soon you'll be finding what you've waited for.

C   Cmaj7   C6   C
For when you sway with her, holding her close,

         Cmaj7   C6   C
She'll be re - luctant to say "adiós."

Verse 2

G7   G7♭9   G9   G7
Latin A - merican kind of ro - mance

         G7♭9   G9   G7
Has to be - gin with this fabulous dance.

C   Cmaj7   C6   C
Wonderful rhythm she'll never resist,

         Cmaj7   C6   C
Here is the part where she'll want to be kissed.

Verse 3

G7*   C*
Diff'rent from any rhumba,   better than any samba,

G7*   C*
Greater than any tango,   wilder than any conga.

Fm   C*
The minute that you begin,   you'll find it beneath your skin

F6 A Dm A7/C♯ Dm/C G7/B F/A G7* C*
Like the hoo - doo   of   a   voo - doo drum.

Fm   C*
It teaches your heart the beat,   then goes to your head and feet

F6 A Dm A7/C♯ Dm/C G7/B F/A G7* C*
Like a shak - er   of   Ja - mai - ca rum.

Chorus 2

    C7   F
You do the Mambo Jambo,

    C7   F
You dance to break of day, day, day, day.

    C7   F
You do the Mambo Jambo,

    C7   F
All night you holler hey, hey! Holay!

Verse 4

Fm   C*
You'll find at the break of day,   your heart has been flown away

F6 A Dm A7/C♯ Dm/C G7/B F/A G7* C*
To a land where on - ly   lov - ers dwell.

Fm   C*
The moment your love is found,   the moment your heart is bound,

F6 A Dm A7/C♯ Dm/C G7/B F/A G7* C*
You will bless the   Mam - bo Jam - bo spell.

A Man and a Woman
(Un Homme et une Femme)
from A MAN AND A WOMAN

Original Words by Pierre Barouh
English Words by Jerry Keller
Music by Francis Lai

Melody:

When hearts are pass-ing in the night,

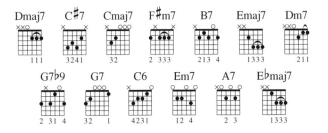

Dmaj7   C#7   Cmaj7   F#m7   B7   Emaj7   Dm7

G7b9   G7   C6   Em7   A7   Ebmaj7

Verse 1

    N.C.   **Dmaj7**
When hearts are passing in the night, in the lonely night,

             C#7
Then they must hold each other tight, oh, so very tight,

              Cmaj7
And take a chance that in the light, in tomorrow's light,

          F#m7 B7   **Emaj7**
They'll stay to - gether.   So much in love.

Verse 2

    N.C.   **Dmaj7**
And in the silence of the morning mist, of the morning mist,

             C#7
When lips are waiting to be kissed, longing to be kissed,

              Cmaj7
Where is the reason to resist and deny a kiss

          F#m7   **B7**   **Emaj7**
That holds a promise   of happi - ness?

Bridge

N.C.   **Dm7 G7♭9**   **Cmaj7**
Though yester - day _____ still sur - rounds you

      Dm7   **G7**   **C6**
With a warm and precious memo - ry,

F#m7 B7   **Emaj7**
Maybe ___ for to - morrow

        Em7   **A7**   **Dmaj7**
We can build a new dream ___ for you and me.

Verse 3

N.C.   **Dmaj7**
This glow we feel is something rare, something really rare.

      C#7
So come and say you want to share,

           Cmaj7
Want to really share the beauty waiting for us there.

                F#m7 B7   **Emaj7**
Calling for us there that only loving ___ can give the heart.

Verse 4

N.C.   **Dmaj7**
When life is passing in the night, in the rushing night,

      C#7
A man, a woman in the night, in the lonely night,

      Cmaj7
Must take a chance that in the light, in tomorrow's light,

        F#m7   **Emaj7**
They'll be to - gether, so much in love.

    F#7   **B7**   **Emaj7**
To - gether, ___ so much in love.

Outro

F#m7   B7   Emaj7
So tell me ___ you're not a - fraid

To take the chance, really take a chance.

E♭maj7 Dmaj7
Let your   heart begin to dance, let it sing and dance

E♭maj7 Emaj7
To the   music of a glance, of a fleeting glance,

E♭maj7 Dmaj7
To the   music of romance, of a new romance.

E♭maj7 Emaj7
Take a   chance.

Song of the Jet

(Samba do Aviao)
from the film COPACABANA PALACE

English Lyric by Gene Lees
Original Text and Music by
Antonio Carlos Jobim

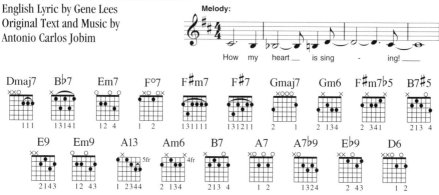

Melody:

How my heart is sing - ing! ___

Dmaj7 Bb7 Em7 F°7 F#m7 F#7 Gmaj7 Gm6 F#m7b5 B7#5
E9 Em9 A13 Am6 B7 A7 A7b9 Eb9 D6

Verse 1

Dmaj7 Bb7   Em7 F°7
How my heart is sing - ing!

F#m7   F#7   Gmaj7
 I see Ri - o de Janei - ro.

Gm6   F#m7   F°7   F#m7b5 B7#5
 My lone - ly, long - ing days are ending.

E9
Rio, my love, there by the sea.

Em9   A13
Rio, my love, waiting ___ for me.

Verse 2

Dmaj7 Bb7   Em7 F°7
See the cable cars ___   that sway

        F#m7   F#7   Gmaj7 Gm6
Above ___ the Bay ___ of Guanaba - ra.

Gmaj7   Gm6
Tiny sailboats far ___ below

Dmaj7   F°7
Dance the samba as ___ they go.

Gmaj7   **Gm6**
Shining Rio, there ____ you lie,

F♯m7 B7♯5   **Em7**   **A13**
City   of sun, of sea and sky,

Am6   **B7**
Mountains of green rising so high.

Gmaj7
Four minutes more,

                    Em7
We'll be there ___ at the airport of Galeao,

E9
Rio de Janeiro, Rio de Janeiro,

A7   **A7♭9**
Rio de Janeiro, Rio de Janeiro,

Verse 3

Dmaj7   **B♭7**   **Em7**   **F°7**   **F♯m7**
Statue of ___ the Sav - ior   with open arms

    F♯7   **Gmaj7 Gm6**
A - bove the yellow sea - shore.

Gmaj7   **Gm6**
Sugar Loaf in maj - esty

Dmaj7   **F°7**
Climbing from a sil - ver sea,

Gmaj7   **Gm6**
Dark eyed girls who smile ___ at me,

F♯m7 B7♯5   **Em7**   **A13**
City   of love and myster - ies.

Am6   **B7**
Fasten seatbelts, no smoking, please.

Gmaj7   **Em7**
Now we are desending and ev - 'rything's rushing,

          E9   **E♭9 D6**
And now the wheels touch the   ground.

Translated Lyrics

Minha alma canta, Vejo o Rio de Janeiro.
Estou morrendo de saudade.
Rio, teu mar, praias sem fim,
Rio, você foi feito pra mim.
Cristo Redentor, braços abertos sobre a Guanabara.
Este samba é só porque,
Rio, eu gusto de você.
A morena vai sambar,
Seu corpo todo balançar.
Rio de sol, de céu, de mar,
Dentro de mais um minute estaremos no Galeão
Cristo Redentor, braços abertos sobre a Guanabara.
Este samba é só porque,
Rio, eu gusto de você.
A morena vai sambar,
Seu corpo todo balançar.
Aperte o cinto, vamos chegar.
Agua brilhando, olha a pista chegando,
E vamos nós,
Aterrar.

Mañana

Words and Music by
Peggy Lee and Dave Barbour

Melody:

The fau-cet she is drip-ping and the

C   C/E   C°7   G7   Am7   Dm7

A7   Dm   A7/E   Dm/F   F#°7   C6

Verse 1

       C   C/E   C°7   G7
The faucet she is dripping and the fence she's falling down.

                      C   Am7   Dm7
My pocket needs some money so I can't go in to town.

G7 C   A7   Dm A7/E Dm/F
My brother isn't working and my sister doesn't care.

F#°7 G7   C
The car she needs a motor so I can't go anywhere.

Chorus 1

G7 C   A7 Dm
Ma - ñana, ma - ñana,

  G7   C6 Dm7 G7
Ma - ñana is soon enough for me.

Verse 2

       C   C/E C°7   G7
My mother's always work - ing, she's working very hard.

                       C   Am7   Dm7
But ev'ry time she looks for me I'm sleeping in the yard.

G7   C   A7   Dm   A7/E Dm/F
My mother thinks I'm lazy and maybe she is right.

F#°7 G7   C
I'll go to work mañana, but I gotta sleep tonight.

Chorus 2   *Repeat Chorus 1*

            C   C/E   C°7   G7

Verse 3   Oh, once I had some money but I gave it to my friend.

                                        C   Am7   Dm7

He said he'd paid me double, it was only for a lend.

G7   C   A7   Dm   A7/E Dm/F

But he said a little later that the horse she was so slow.

      F#°7 G7   C

Why he   gave the horse my money is something I don't know.

Chorus 3   *Repeat Chorus 1*

            C   C/E   C°7   G7

Verse 4   My brother took his suitcase and he went away to school.

                                 C   Am7 Dm7

My father said he only learned to be a silly fool.

G7 C   A7   Dm   A7/E Dm/F

My father said that I should learn to make a chili   pot.

F#°7 G7   C

But then I burned the house down, the chili was too hot.

Chorus 4   *Repeat Chorus 1*

            C   C/E   C°7   G7

Verse 5   The window she is broken and the rain is coming in.

                               C   Am7   Dm7

If someone doesn't fix it, I'll be soaking to my skin.

G7 C   A7   Dm   A7/E Dm/F

But if we wait a day or two the rain may go a - way.

F#°7 G7   C

And we don't need a window on such a sunny day.

            G7 C   A7 Dm

Chorus 5   Ma - ñana, ma - ñana,

            G7   C6

Ma - ñana is soon enough for me.

Más Que Nada

Words and Music by
Jorge Ben

Am7   D7   Dm7   E7sus4   E7#9   E7#5   G7   C6   D7/F#   G7/F

Chorus

> Am7 D7 Am7 D7 Dm7   D7   Am7
> Oo, _____ when your eyes meet mine,
>
> E7sus4   Am7 D7 Am7 D7
> Pow! Pow! Pow!
>
> Am7 D7 Am7 D7 Dm7   D7   Am7
> Oo, _____ I could lose my mind.
>
> E7sus4   Am7
> Ow! Ow! Ow!

Verse

> E7#9   Am7   E7#9
>   It's a feel - ing that begins to grow an' grow
>
>   Am7
> An' grow inside ____ of me
>
>   E7#9   Am7
> 'Til I feel like I'm gonna explode.
>
>   E7#5   Am7 D7
> Oh, this is what you do to me!

Am7 D7		Dm7		G7			C6

Am7 D7   Dm7   G7   C6
Are your lips ____ saying things ____ that you feel in your heart?

D7/F♯   G7/F   E7♯9   Am7
If your heart is beating madly,   then let the music start.

E7♯9   Am7
Hold me, hold ____ me!

  E7♯9   Am7
It's heaven, ooh, it's heaven when you hold me.

  E7♯9   Am7
I want you night and day.

    E7♯5   Am7 D7 Am7 D7 Am
Ooh, I want you here to stay.

Translated Lyrics

Chorus   O ariá raiô ôbá, ôbá, ôbá.

Verse   Más que nada said a minha
Frente que eu quero pasar,
Pois o samba está animado,
O que eu quero e sambar.
Esse samba que é mixto de maracatú
E samba de preto vellho, samba de preto tú.
Más que nada, um samba como esse tao legal,
Você nao vai querer que eu chegue no final.

Meditation
(Meditacão)

Music by Antonio Carlos Jobim
Original Words by Newton Mendonça
English Words by Norman Gimbel

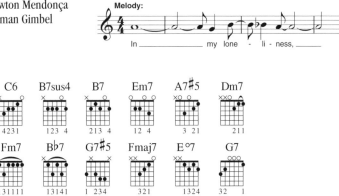

C6   B7sus4   B7   Em7   A7#5   Dm7   Fm7   Bb7   G7#5   Fmaj7   E°7   G7

Verse 1

    C6   **B7sus4** **B7**
In my lone - liness,

                C6
When you're gone ____ and I'm all by myself

            Em7   **A7#5**
And I need your ____ caress,

Dm7   **Fm7**   **Bb7**
I just think ____ of you.

            Em7   **A7#5**
And the thought ____ of you holding me near

       Dm7   **G7#5**
Makes my lone - liness soon disappear.

Verse 2

C6   B7sus4   B7
Though you're far ___ away,

        C6
I have on - ly to close my eyes

              Em7   A7$\sharp$5
And you are back ___ to stay.

Dm7   Fm7   B$\flat$7
I just close ___ my eyes

          Em7   A7$\sharp$5
And the sad - ness that missing you brings

          Dm7   G7$\sharp$5
Soon is gone ___ and this heart of mine sings.

Bridge

Fmaj7   Fm7   B$\flat$7
Yes, I love ___ you so

        Em7   E$\flat$°7   Dm7 G7$\sharp$5
And that ___ for me is all ___ I need to know.

Verse 3

C6   B7sus4   B7
I will wait ___ for you

        C6
Till the sun ___ falls from out of the sky

          Em7   A7$\sharp$5
For what else can ___ I do?

Dm7   Fm7   B$\flat$7
I will wait ___ for you,

     Em7   A7$\sharp$5   Dm7
Meditat - ing how sweet ___ life will be

          G7   C6 (G7$\sharp$5)
When you come ___ back to me.

More
(Ti Guarderò Nel Cuore)
from the film MONDO CANE

Music by Nino Oliviero and Riz Ortolani
Italian Lyrics by Marcello Ciorciolini
English Lyrics by Norman Newell

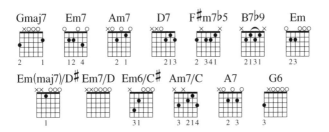

Verse 1

> Gmaj7   Em7   Am7   D7
> More than the greatest love the world has known,
>
> Gmaj7 Em7   Am7 D7
> This is the love I'll give you a - lone.
>
> Gmaj7   Em7   Am7 D7
> More than the simple words I try to say,
>
> Gmaj7 Em7   Am7   F#m7♭5 B7♭9
> I only   live to love you more each day.

Chorus 1

> Em   Em(maj7)/D#
> More than you'll ever know,
>
>   Em7/D   Em6/C#
> My arms long to hold you so.
>
>   Am7/C A7
> My life will be in your keeping,
>
> Am7   D7
> Waking, sleeping, laughing, weeping.

Verse 2

Gmaj7   Em7   Am7   D7
Longer than always is a long, long time

Gmaj7   Em7   Am7   F#m7b5 B7b9
But far be - yond forever you'll be mine.

Chorus 2

Em   Em(maj7)/D#
I know I never lived

Em7/D   Em6/C#   Am7/C
Be - fore and my heart is very sure

Am7   D7   G6
No one else could love you more.

Noche de Ronda
(Be Mine Tonight)

Original Words and Music by Maria Teresa Lara
English Words by Sunny Skylar

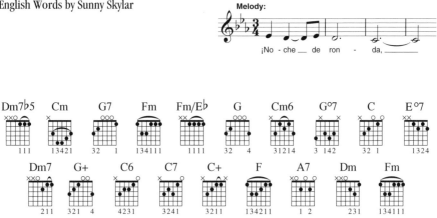

Dm7♭5   Cm   G7   Fm   Fm/E♭   G   Cm6   G°7   C   E°7

Dm7   G+   C6   C7   C+   F   A7   Dm   Fm

Verse 1

        N.C.   **Dm7♭5 Cm**
        ¡Noche de ron - da,

        Dm7♭5   **Cm**
          Qué triste pasas,

        Dm7♭5   **Cm**   **Dm7♭5 G7**
          Qué triste cruzas por mi bal - cón!

        Fm   **Fm/E♭**
        Noche de ron - da,

        Dm7♭5   **Fm Fm/E♭**
          Cómo me hie - res,

        Dm7♭5   **Fm**   **Dm7♭5 G Cm6 G°7 G7**
          Cómo las - timas mi cora - zón.

GUITAR CHORD SONGBOOK

Verse 2

N.C.   **Dm7♭5 Cm**
Noche de ron - da,

Dm7♭5   Cm
  The night is waking.

Dm7♭5   Cm   Dm7♭5 G Cm6 G°7 G7
  My arms are aching to hold you near.

Chorus

N.C.   **C**
See the setting sun, the evening's just begun

               E♭°7 G7
And love is in the air. Be mine to - night.

N.C.   **G7**
At a time like this, would you refuse the kiss

              Dm7 G7   **G+ C6**
I'm begging you to share? ____ Be mine to - night.

N.C.   **C**
Promise this, my own, before the night has flown,

               C7 C+ F A7
You'll tell me that you care and hold me tight.

Dm   Fm   Cm
  Whisper love words, oh, so tender,

     G7   Cm
Give your kisses in sur - render,

     G7   Cm
Let your heart be mine to - night.

Translated Lyrics

Chorus

¡Luna que se
Quiebra sobre la tiniebla de mi soledad!
¿Adondevas?
¿Dime si esta noche tú le vas
De ronda como ella se fue,
Con quien está?
Dile que la quiero, dile que me
Muero de tanto esperar,
Que vuelva ya, que las rondas
No son buenas, que hacen daño,
Que dan penas, que se acaba por llorar.

Once I Loved

(Amor em Paz) (Love in Peace)

Music by Antonio Carlos Jobim
Portuguese Lyrics by Vinicius de Moraes
English Lyrics by Ray Gilbert

Verse 1

> **Gm7 C7#5   Fmaj7**
> Once _____ I loved,
>
> **F#°7   Gm7   G#°7**
> And I gave so much to this love,
>
> **   Am7**
> You were the world to me.
>
> **Fm7 Bb7#5   Ebmaj7**
> Once _____ I cried
>
> **   Em7b5   A7b9**
> At the thought I was foolish and proud
>
> **   Dmaj7   D7b9**
> And let you say goodbye.

Gm7 C7#5   Fmaj7

Verse 2   Then _____ one day,

F#°7   Gm7   G#°7

    From my infinite sadness you came

                Am7

And brought me love again.

Fm7 Bb7#5   Ebmaj7

Now _____ I know

      Em7b5   A7b9

That no matter whatever be - falls

       Dmaj7

I'll never let you go.

G7   Cmaj7 F7   Bbmaj7

Verse 3   I will hold you close, _____ make you stay.

       B°7   Bbm6   Am7

Because love is the saddest thing when it goes away,

Ab7b5   G7   Gm7 A7b9*   Dm6   (D7)

    Because love is the saddest thing _____ when it goes away.

Translated Lyrics

Verse 1   Eu amei E amei muito mais do que devia amar
               E chorei ao sentir que eu iria sofrer e me dese perar.

Verse 2   Fol, então que da minha infinita trizteza aconteceu você
               Elcontrei em você a razão de vi vir e de amar em paz.

Verse 3   E não sofrer mais nunca mais
               Porque o amor é a coisa mais triste quando se destaz
               O amor é a coisa triste quando se desfaz.

One Note Samba

(Samba de Uma Nota So)

Original Lyrics by Newton Mendonça
English Lyrics by Antonio Carlos Jobim
Music by Antonio Carlos Jobim

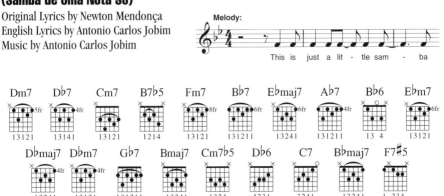

Dm7 Db7 Cm7 B7b5 Fm7 Bb7 Ebmaj7 Ab7 Bb6 Ebm7

Dbmaj7 Dbm7 Gb7 Bmaj7 Cm7b5 Db6 C7 Bbmaj7 F7#5

Verse 1

       Dm7   Db7   Cm7   B7b5
This is just a little sam - ba built up - on a single note.

       Dm7   Db7   Cm7   B7b5
Other notes are bound to fol - low but the root is still that note.

       Fm7   Bb7
Now this new one is the con - sequence

       Ebmaj7   Ab7
Of the one we've just been through,

       Dm7   Db7   Cm7   B7b5   Bb6
As I'm bound to be the un - avoidable consequence ___ of you.

Bridge

   E♭m7   A♭7
There's so many people who can talk and talk and talk

        D♭maj7
And just say nothing, or nearly nothing.

   D♭m7   G♭7
I have used up all the scale I know,

                    Bmaj7   Cm7♭5 B7♭5
And at the end I've come to nothing, or nearly nothing.

Verse 2

    Dm7   D♭7   Cm7   B7♭5
So I come back to my first ___ note, as I must come back to you.

    Dm7   D♭7   Cm7   B7♭5
I will pour into that one ___ note all the love I feel for you.

    Fm7   B♭7
Any - one who wants the whole ___ show:

    E♭maj7   A♭7
Re, Mi, Fa, Sol, La, Ti, Do,

    D♭6   C7
He will find himself with no ___ show.

     B♭maj7   B♭6 (F7♯5)
Better play ___ the note you know.

Only Trust Your Heart

Words by Sammy Cahn
Music by Benny Carter

Nev - er trust the stars _____ when you're a - bout

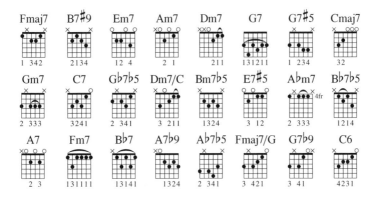

Verse 1

    Fmaj7   B7#9   Em7   Am7
Never trust the stars when you're a - bout to fall in love.

    Dm7   G7 G7#5   Cmaj7   Gm7 C7
Look for hidden signs ___ before you start to sigh.

    Fmaj7   B7#9   Em7   Am7
Never trust the moon when you're a - bout to taste his kiss.

    Dm7   G7 G7#5   C7   Gm7
He knows all the lines, ___ and he knows how to lie.

Bridge

G♭7♭5 Fmaj7 Am7   Dm7
Just wait _____ for a night

Dm7/C   Bm7♭5   E7♯5
When the skies are all bare,

     Am7 A♭m7 Gm7 C7
Then, if you still   care,

Verse 2

Fmaj7   B7♯9   Em7   Am7
Never trust your dream when you're a - bout to fall in love,

Dm7   G7 G7♯5   B♭7♭5 A7
For your dream will quick - ly fall a - part.

   Dm7   Fm7 B♭7 Cmaj7   Em7 A7♭9
So, if you're smart, ____   really smart,

A♭7♭5   Fmaj7/G G7♭9 C6
Only trust _____ your   heart.

Poinciana
(Song of the Tree)

Words by Buddy Bernier
Music by Nat Simon

Melody:

Poin - ci - an - a, _____ your branch - es

D13   Am7   D7   G6   Gmaj9   Dm7

G7   Cm7   Gmaj7   Dmaj7   D6

Intro

D13	Am7	D13	Am7
D13	D7	G6	
D13	Am7	D13	Am7
D13	D7	G6

Verse 1

D13   Gmaj9   Dm7 G7
Poinci - ana, your branches speak to me of love,
Cm7   Gmaj7 G6
Pale moon is casting shadows from a - bove.

Verse 2

Am7 D13   Gmaj9   Dm7
   Poinci - ana, somehow I feel the jungle heat,
G7   Cm7   Gmaj7 G6 Gmaj7 G6
   With - in me there grows a rhythmic savage beat.

	Cm7 Dmaj7 D6
Bridge	Love is ev'rywhere, it's magic perfume fills the air.

Bridge

Cm7   **Dmaj7 D6**
Love is ev'rywhere, it's magic perfume fills the air.

Cm7   **Am7**
To and fro you sway, my heart's in time, I've learned to care.

Verse 3

D13   Gmaj9   Dm7 G7
 Poinci - ana, though skies may turn from blue to gray,

Cm7   Gmaj7
My love will live forever and a day.

Quiet Nights of Quiet Stars

(Corcovado)

English Words by Gene Lees
Original Words and Music by
Antonio Carlos Jobim

Melody:

Qui - et nights of qui - et stars,

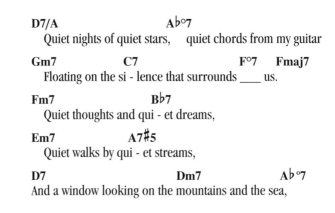

Verse 1

D7/A		A♭°7	

Quiet nights of quiet stars,   quiet chords from my guitar

Gm7   C7   F°7   Fmaj7

Floating on the si - lence that surrounds ____ us.

Fm7   B♭7

Quiet thoughts and qui - et dreams,

Em7   A7♯5

Quiet walks by qui - et streams,

D7   Dm7   A♭°7

And a window looking on the mountains and the sea,

How lovely!

Verse 2

     D7/A   **A♭°7**
     This is where I want to be.   Here, with you so close to me,

       Gm7   **C7**   **F°7** **Fmaj7**
Until ____ the final flicker of life's em - ber.

Fm7   **B♭7♭5**
     I, who was lost and lonely,

Em7   **Am7** **Dm7**   **G7♭9**
     Believing life was only   a bitter, tragic joke,

              Em7 **Dm7**   **G7**
Have found with you, ____   the meaning of ex - istence.

      C6
Oh, my love.

Quizás, Quizás, Quizás
(Perhaps, Perhaps, Perhaps)

Music and Spanish Words by Osvaldo Farres
English Words by Joe Davis

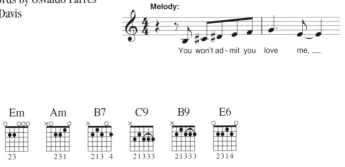

Em   Am   B7   C9   B9   E6

Verse 1

N.C.   Em
You won't admit you love me,

     Am B7   Em   Am
And so,   how am I ever to know?

B7   Em   C9   B9   Em
You always tell me, "Per - haps, per - haps, per - haps."

Verse 2

N.C.   Em
A million times I've asked you,

     Am B7   Em   Am
And then I ask you over a - gain.

B7   Em   C9   B9   Em Am
You only answer, "Per - haps, per - haps, per - haps."

	Em	B7	E6

Bridge   If you can't make your mind up, we'll never get started,

                     B7   **E6**
And I don't want to wind up being parted, broken - hearted.

                    N.C.   **Em**   **Am**

Verse 3   So, if you really love me, say "yes,"

               B7   **Em**   **Am**
But if you don't, dear, con - fess,

               B7   **Em**   **C9**   **B9**   **Em Am Em**
And please don't tell me, "Per - haps, per - haps, per - haps."

Translated Lyrics

Verse 1   Siempre que te pregunto que cuando como y donde,
             Tu siempre nie respondes "quizás, quizás, quizás."

Verse 2   Y así pason los días y yo desesperado y tú,
             Tú contestando "quizás, quizás, quizás."

Bridge   Estás perdiendo el tiempo pensando, pensando;
             Por lo que mast tú quieras hasta cuando, hasta cuando.

Verse 4   Y así pasan los días y yo desesperado y tú,
             Tú contestando "quizás, quizás, quizás."

Samba de Orfeu

Words by Antonio Maria
Music by Luiz Bonfa

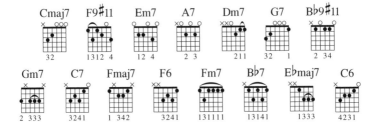

Verse 1

N.C.   **Cmaj7**
Quero viver, ____ quero sambar.

               F9♯11 **Em7**
Até sentir a essên - cia da vi - da,

A7   **Dm7**
  Me falta - ar.

G7   **Dm7** **G7**   **Dm7**
  Quero sambar, ____ quero viver.

G7   **Dm7**
  Depois do sam - ba,

            G7   **Bb9♯11** **A7**
Tá bem meu a - mor posso morrer.

Verse 2   *Repeat Verse 1*

Bridge

        Gm7 C7   **Fmaj7 F6**
Quem quizer _____ gostar de mim,

Fmaj7   Fm7 Bb7   **Ebmaj7**
Se quizer _____ vai ser assim.

Dm7   G7   Cmaj7
Vamos   viver, ___ vamos sambar.

Verse 3

Cmaj7   **F9$\sharp$11**
Se a fantasia rasgar, meu amor,

Em7   A7   Dm7
Cu com - pro ou - tra.

G7   **Dm7 G7**   **Dm7**
Vamos sambar, ___ vamos viver.

G7   **Dm7**
O samba é ___ livre,

            G7   **C6**
Eu sou livre tam - bem, até morrer.

Say "Sí, Sí"

Music by Ernesto Lecuona
Spanish Words by Francia Luban
English Words by Al Stillman

Melody:

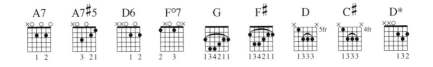

In   Spain they __ say __

A7   A7#5   D6   F°7   G   F#   D   C#   D*

Verse 1

      A7
In Spain they say "Sí, sí,"

A7#5 D6   **A7#5 D6**
In   France you'll hear "Oui, oui."

           A7
Ev'ry little Dutch girl says "Ya, ya,"

          D6   **A7#5 D6**
Ev'ry little Danish doll says "Da."

F°7 A7
But,   sweetheart, tell me why,

A7#5 D6   **A7#5 D6**
No   matter how I   try,

           G   **F#**
You won't listen to my plea,

G   **D C# D**
Won't say "yes" in any lan - guage to me?

F°7 A7   **D***
When will you say "Sí, sí?"

GUITAR CHORD SONGBOOK

Verse 2

A7
In Hindustan "Ug, ug!"

A7#5   D6   A7#5   D6
Means "O.K., babe, let's   hug."

            A7
Never was a Panama ma

                  D6   A7#5   D6
Who told her Trini - daddy, "No can   do!"

F°7   A7
On   ev'ry Virgin Isle

A7#5   D6   A7#5   D6
They   say it with a   smile.

                  G   F#
But you never hear my plea,

G   D   C#   D
Won't say "yes" in any lan - guage to me.

F°7   A7   D*
When will you say "Sí, sí?"

She's a Carioca

Lyric by Ray Gilbert
Music by Antonio Carlos Jobim
Portugese Lyric by Vinicius De Moraes

Melody:

Tup - tup - tup, peet-a doon ba, ___ peet - a

G6   Gm6   F#m7   F°7   E7   A7   Dmaj7   Gm7   Bm7add4   Em7

C°7   G#m7   Am7   D7   Dmaj9   C#7#9   Cmaj7   B7#9   Bb6   Bb9

Verse

        G6   **Gm6**
        Tup-tup-tup, peet-a doon ba, peet-a doon ba, peet-a doon.

        F#m7   **F°7**
        Tup-tup-tup, peet-a doon ba, peet-a doon ba.

                        E7 A7   **Dmaj7 Gm7**
        Here she comes. ____   Here she comes.

                Dmaj7   **Bm7add4**
        Ela e carioca. She's a carioca.

        E7
            Just see the way she walks.

        Em7   **C°7**   **G#m7 E7**   **A7**
            Nobody else can be what she is _____ to me.

            Am7   **D7**   **E7**   **Gm6**
        I look and what do I see when I look deep in her eyes?

            Dmaj9 C#7#9   **Cmaj7   B7#9**
        I can see the sea, a for - gotten   road,

                    Bb6   **D7**
            The ca - ressing skies.

B♭9   Dmaj7   Bm7add4
And not only that, I'm in love with her

E7
The most exciting way.

Em7   C°7   G♯m7 E7   A7
It's written on my lips where her kis - ses stay.

   Am7   D7   E7   Gm6
She smiles and all of a sudden the world is smiling for me.

      Dmaj9 C♯7♯9   Cmaj7 C♯7♯9   Dmaj9
And you know what else? She's a cari - oca. Ela e carioca.

E7   Gm6
Tup-tup-tup, peet-a doon ba, peet-a doon ba, peet-a doon.

F♯m7   F°7
Tup-tup-tup, peet-a doon ba, peet-a doon ba.

          E7 A7   Dmaj7
There she goes. ____ There she goes.

Slightly Out of Tune

(Desafinado)

English Lyric by Jon Hendricks and Jessie Cavanaugh
Original Text by Newton Mendonça
Music by Antonio Carlos Jobim

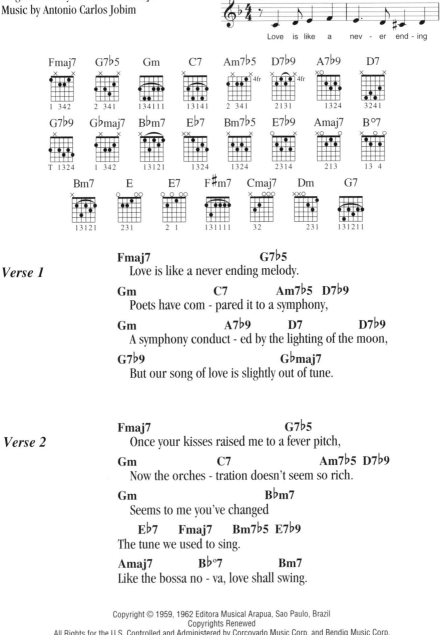

Melody:

Love is like a nev - er end - ing

Verse 1

Fmaj7   G7♭5
Love is like a never ending melody.

Gm   C7   Am7♭5 D7♭9
Poets have com - pared it to a symphony,

Gm   A7♭9   D7   D7♭9
A symphony conduct - ed by the lighting of the moon,

G7♭9   G♭maj7
But our song of love is slightly out of tune.

Verse 2

Fmaj7   G7♭5
Once your kisses raised me to a fever pitch,

Gm   C7   Am7♭5 D7♭9
Now the orches - tration doesn't seem so rich.

Gm   B♭m7
Seems to me you've changed

E♭7 Fmaj7 Bm7♭5 E7♭9
The tune we used to sing.

Amaj7   B♭°7   Bm7
Like the bossa no - va, love shall swing.

Bridge

E   Amaj7   B♭°7   Bm7   E7
We used to harmonize, ____ two souls in perfect time.

Amaj7   F♯m7   Bm7   E7
   Now the song is diff'rent and the words don't even rhyme.

     Cmaj7   B♭°7   Dm   G7
'Cause you forgot the melody our hearts would always croon,

       Gm   D7♭9   G7   C7
And so what good's a heart that's slightly out of tune?

Verse 3

Fmaj7   G7♭5
   Tune your heart to mine the way it used to be,

Gm   C7   Am7♭5   D7♭9
   Join with me in harmony and sing a song of loving.

     Gm   B♭m7   E♭7   Fmaj7   Dm
We're bound to get in tune a - gain be - fore too long.

       G7
There'll be no desafinado

          B♭m7   E♭7
When your heart be - longs to me completely.

       G7   Gm
Then you won't be slightly out of tune,

      C7   Fmaj7
You'll sing a - long with me.

Só Danço Samba

(Jazz 'n' Samba)
from the film COPACABANA PALACE

English Lyric by Norman Gimbel
Original Text by Vinicius de Moraes
Music by Antonio Carlos Jobim

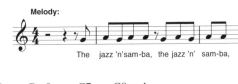

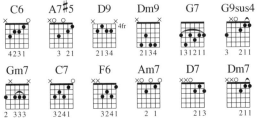

Verse 1

       C6   A7#5
The jazz 'n' samba, the jazz 'n' samba,

       D9
    Hear it all around.

       Dm9   G7   C6
The jazz 'n' samba, the jazz 'n' samba sound.

Verse 2

       G9sus4 C6   A7#5
    The jazz 'n' samba, the jazz 'n' samba,

       D9
    Swingin' soft and low.

       Dm9   G7   C6
The jazz 'n' samba, the jazz 'n' samba go!

	Gm7 C7 F6

Bridge

> **Gm7**   **C7**   **F6**
> Jet from Rio, non - stop U.S.A.
>
> **Am7**   **D7**
> This new sound came one day
>
>   **Dm7**   **G7**
> And it's clear that it's here to stay.

Verse 3

>   **C6**   **A7#5**
> It's jazz 'n' samba, it's so refreshing,
>
> **D9**
>   Like a new perfume.
>
>   **Dm9**   **G7**   **C6**
> It's jazz 'n' samba, it's jazz 'n' samba,   ummm!

Translated Lyrics

Verse

Só danço samba, só danço samba.
Vai, vai, vai, vai, vai.
Só danço samba, só danço samba. Vai.

Bridge

Já dancei o twist até demais.
Mas não sei me cansei
Do calypso ao chá chá chá.

So Nice
(Summer Samba)

Original Words and Music by
Marcos Valle and Paulo Sergio Valle
English Words by Norman Gimbel

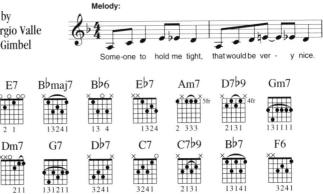

Fmaj7   Bm7   E7   Bbmaj7   Bb6   Eb7   Am7   D7b9   Gm7

Em7b5   A7#5   Dm7   G7   Db7   C7   C7b9   Bb7   F6

Verse 1

Fmaj7
Someone to hold me tight, that would be very nice.

Bm7   **E7**
Someone to love me right, that would be very nice.

Bbmaj7   **Bb6**
Someone to understand each little dream in me,

Eb7
Someone to take my hand, to be a team with me.

Am7   **D7b9**   **Gm7**
 So nice, ___ life would be so nice

Em7b5 A7#5   **Dm7**
 If one day I'd find

G7   **Gm7**
 Someone who would take my hand

                   Db7   **C7**
And samba thru life ___ with me.

Verse 2

Fmaj7
Someone to cling to me, stay with me right or wrong,

Bm7   **E7**
Someone to sing to me, some little samba song.

B♭maj7   **B♭6**
Someone to take my heart, then give his heart to me.

E♭7
Someone who's ready to give love a start with me.

Am7   **D7♭9**   **Gm7 C7♭9**
   Oh, yes, ___ that would be so nice.

Fmaj7   **B♭7**   **F6**
Should it be you and me, I could see it would be nice.

Someone to Light Up My Life
(Se Todos Fossem Iguais a Voce)

English Lyric by Gene Lees
Original Text by Vinicius de Moraes
Music by Antonio Carlos Jobim

Melody:

Where shall I look for the

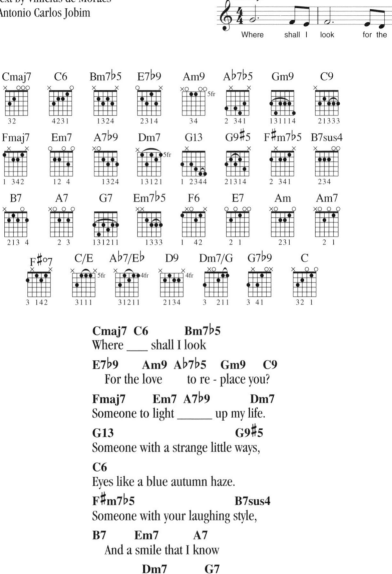

Verse 1

Cmaj7 C6　　**Bm7♭5**
Where ____ shall I look

E7♭9　　**Am9 A♭7♭5 Gm9**　　**C9**
For the love　　to re - place you?

Fmaj7　　**Em7 A7♭9**　　**Dm7**
Someone to light _____ up my life.

G13　　　　　　　**G9♯5**
Someone with a strange little ways,

C6
Eyes like a blue autumn haze.

F♯m7♭5　　　　　　**B7sus4**
Someone with your laughing style,

B7　　**Em7**　　**A7**
And a smile that I know

　　　　Dm7　　**G7**
Will keep haunting me endlessly.

Verse 2

Cmaj7 C6   Bm7♭5
Some - times in stars

E7♭9   Am9 A♭7♭5   Gm9 C9
 Or the swift   flight of sea birds,

Fmaj7 Em7♭5 A7♭9   Fmaj7 F6 Fmaj7 F6 E7
I catch a moment _____ of you.

Am   Am7   F♯°7
That's why I walk all a - lone,

Cmaj7   F♯m7♭5   C/E A♭7/E♭
Searching for something un - known.

D9   Dm7/G   G7♭9   C
Searching for something or someone to light up my life.

Translated Lyrics

Verse 1

Se todos fossem iguais a você,
Que maravi lha viver.
Uma canção pelo ar,
Uma cidade a cantar,
Uma mulher a cantar a sorrir;
A pedir, a cantar, a belezade amar.

Verse 2

Como o sol como a flor, como a luz.
Amar sem mentir nem sofrer.
Exiztiria a verdade, verdade que ninguem vê,
Se todos fossem no mundo iguais a você.

Sway
(Quien Será)

English Words by Norman Gimbel
Spanish Words and Music by
Pablo Beltran Ruiz

Melody:

When ma-rim-ba rhy-thms start to play,

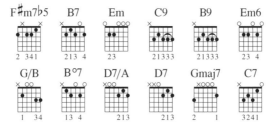

F#m7b5 B7 Em C9 B9 Em6

G/B B°7 D7/A D7 Gmaj7 C7

Verse 1

N.C.   F#m7b5 B7
When marimba rhythms start to   play,

F#m7b5 B7 Em
Dance with me, make me sway.

                    C9   B9
Like the lazy ocean hugs the shore,

C9   B9 Em6
Hold me close, sway me more.

Verse 2

                    F#m7b5 B7
Like a flower bending in the   breeze,

F#m7b5 B7 Em
Bend with me, sway with ease.

                        C9   B9
When we dance you have a way with me,

C9   B9 Em6
Stay with me, sway with me.

	G/B Bb°7 D7/A D7

Bridge   Other dancers may be on the floor, dear,

                 Gmaj7
But my eyes will see only you.

                 B7
Only you have that magic technique,

                       Em C7
When we sway I grow weak.

           B7   **F#m7b5 B7**

Verse 3   I can hear the sound of vio   -   lins,

F#m7b5 B7 Em
Long be - fore it begins.

                      C9   **B9**
Make me thrill as only you know how,

C9   **B9**   **Em6**
Sway me smooth, sway me now.

B7   **Em**
   Sway me smooth, sway me now.

Translated Lyrics

Verse 1   Quien será la que me quiera a mi,
Quien será quien será.
Quien será la que me dé su amor,
Quien será quien será.

Verse 2   Yo no sé si la podré encontrar,
Yo no sé yo no sé.
Yo no sé si volré a querer,
Yo no sé yo no sé.

Bridge   He querido volver a viver,
La pasión y el calor de otro amor.
De otro amor que me hiciera sentir,
Que me hiciera feliz como ayer lo.

Verse 3   Fuí quien será la que me quiera a mí,
Quien será quien será.
Quien será la que me dé su amor,
Quien será quien será quien será, quien será.

Telephone Song

English Words by Norman Gimbel
Portuguese Words by Ronaldo Boscoli
Music by Roberto Menescal

Melody:

Buzz, buzz, line is bus-y ev-'ry time that I phone.

Dm7   G7   Gm7   C7   Fmaj7   E7   Am7   D7   F#m7♭5   B7#9

Em7   B7   Em7♭5   A7   Fm7   B♭7   E♭m7   A♭7   C6

Verse 1

      Dm7   G7   Dm7
Buzz, buzz, line is busy ev'ry time that I phone.

G7   Dm7   G7   Dm7
Buzz, ____ he's the longest talker I've ever known.

G7   Gm7   C7   Gm7
Buzz, buzz, I've been trying now to reach him all day.

C7   Gm7   C7   Gm7   C7
Buzz, ____ when I get him I'll for - get what to say.

Fmaj7   E7   Am7
(Should I call the oper - ator?)

D7   Dm7
(Is the number that I gave him my own?)

Verse 2

G7   Dm7   G7   Dm7
Buzz, buzz, I've been sitting here and dialing all day.

G7   Dm7   G7   Dm7
Buzz, ____ got to get him and there must be a way.

G7   Gm7   C7   Gm7
Buzz, buzz, if you heard the way he begged me to call.

C7   Gm7   C7   Gm7   C7
Buzz, ____ you could never under - stand it at all.

Fmaj7   **E7**   **Am7**
(When I met him he was quiet,

F♯m7♭5 **B7♯9**   **Em7**
But now he learned to talk.)

    F♯m7♭5   **B7**   **Em7**
Buzz, buzz, think I'm going to give ____ up.

F♯m7♭5 **B7♯9**   **Em7**
Can't   stand it any - more.

        Dm7   **G7**   **Em7♭5**   **A7**

Verse 3   Buzz, buzz, I've de - cided that our romance is through.

Fm7   **B♭7** **Em7♭5**   **A7**
Can it be true? The phone is ringing!

E♭m7   **A♭7**   **Dm7**   **G7**   **C6**
I can't be - lieve it! Wait till I say, "Hel - lo!"

Translated Lyrics

Verse 1   Tuem, tuem, ocupado decima vez.
Tuem, telefono e não consigo falar.
Tuem, tuem estou ou vindo há muito mais de um mês.
Tuem, já começa quando eu penso em discar.
(Eu já estou descomfiando.)
Que ela deu meu telephone p'ra mim.)

Verse 2   Tuem, tuem, e dizer que a vida in teira esperei.
Tuem, qui dei duro e me matei p'ra encontrar.
Tuem, tuem tôda alista quase que eu decorei
Tuem, dia e miote não parei de discar.
(E só vendo com que jeito. Pedia p'ra eu ligar.)
Tuem, tuem, não entendo mais nada.
P'ra que é que eu fui topar.

Verse 3   Tuem, tuem, não me diga que agora atendeu.
¿Será, que eu? ¡Eu comsequi, agora encontrar!
A moça atendeu, "Alo."

Tico Tico
(Tico Tico No Fuba)

Words and Music by Zequinha Abreu,
Aloysio Oliveira and Ervin Drake

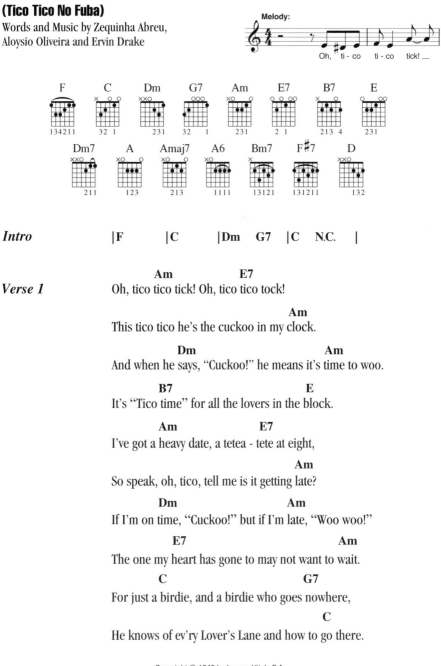

Melody:

Oh, ti - co   ti - co   tick! —

| Intro | |F |C |Dm   G7 |C   N.C. | |

Verse 1

                        Am   **E7**
Oh, tico tico tick! Oh, tico tico tock!

                                 Am
This tico tico he's the cuckoo in my clock.

               Dm   **Am**
And when he says, "Cuckoo!" he means it's time to woo.

               B7   **E**
It's "Tico time" for all the lovers in the block.

               Am   **E7**
I've got a heavy date, a tetea - tete at eight,

                                   Am
So speak, oh, tico, tell me is it getting late?

               Dm   **Am**
If I'm on time, "Cuckoo!" but if I'm late, "Woo woo!"

               E7   **Am**
The one my heart has gone to may not want to wait.

               C   **G7**
For just a birdie, and a birdie who goes nowhere,

                                 C
He knows of ev'ry Lover's Lane and how to go there.

<pre>
                              Dm   G7
          For in affairs of the heart, my tico's terribly smart,

                                       C
          He tells me, "Gently, sentimently at the start!"

          G7   C   G7
             Oh, oh, I hear my little tico tico calling,

                                           C
          Because the time is right and shades of night are falling.
                      Dm   C
          I love that not so cuckoo cuckoo in the clock.

          Dm7   G7   C
          Tico, tico, tico, tico, tock.
</pre>

<pre>
Interlude |A   Amaj7 |A6   A |A6   A |Bm7   E7 |
             |Bm7   E7 |Bm7   E7 |Bm7   E7 |A6   A |
             | Amaj7 |A6   A |F#7 |Bm7 |
             | D |A |E7 |A |
</pre>

Verse 2   *Repeat Verse 1*

Translated Lyrics

O tico tico tá, tá, outra vez aqui,
O tico tico tá comendo o meu fubá.
Si o tico tico tem, tem que se alimentar,
Que vá comer umas minhocas no pomar.
O tico tico tá, tá outra vez aqui,
O tico tico tá comendo o meu fubá.
Eu sei que elle vem viver no meu quintal,
E vem com ares de cañario e de pardal.
Mas por favor tira esse bicho fo celeiro,
Por que elle acaba comendo o fubá inteiro.
Tira esse tico de lá, de cima do meu fubá.
Tem tanta fruta que elle pode pinicar.
Eu já fiz tudo par aver se conseguia.
Botei alpiste para ver si elle comia.
Botei um gato um espantolho e um alçapão,
Mas elle acha que o fubá é que é boa alimentação.

Triste

By Antonio Carlos Jobim

Melody:

Sad __ is to live in sol - tude _____

Cmaj7   A♭maj7   D♭7♭5   Em7   A7   Dm7   Bm7♭5

E7   Am7   B7♯9   Emaj7   F♯m7   B7   G7

Cm7   F7   Gm7   C7   Fmaj7   B♭7   D7

Verse 1

Cmaj7   **A♭maj7 D♭7♭5**
Sad is to live in solitude

Cmaj7   **Em7 A7**
Far from your tranquil altitude.

Dm7   **Bm7♭5**   **E7**   **Am7**
Sad it is to know ____ that no ____ one ev - er

                              B7♯9   **Emaj7**
Can live on a dream ____ that nev - er can be,

F♯m7   **B7**
Will never be.

         Em7   **A7**   **Dm7**   **G7**
Dream - er awake, ____ wake ____ up and see.

	Cmaj7	Cm7 F7

Verse 2

Cmaj7   **Cm7 F7**
Your beauty is an aeroplane

Cmaj7   **Gm7 C7**
So high, my heart can't bear the strain.

Fmaj7   **B♭7**
A heart that stops when you ____ pass by

 Em7   Am7   **D7**
On - ly to cause me pain.

Dm7   **G7** **Cm7 F7 Cm7 F7 Cm7 F7 Cm7 F7**
Sad is to live in sol - itude.

Translated Lyrics

Verse 1   Triste é viver a na solidão
        Na dor cruel de uma paixão
        Triste é saber que ninguem pade viver de ilusão
        Que nunca vai ser, nunca dar
        O sonhador tem que acordar.

Verse 2   Tua beleze é um auiao
        Demals pra um pobre coracao
        Que para pr ate ver passer
        So pra se maltratar
        Triste é viver na solidãd.

Vivo Sonhando
(Dreamer)

Words and Music by Antonio Carlos Jobim
English Lyrics by Gene Lees

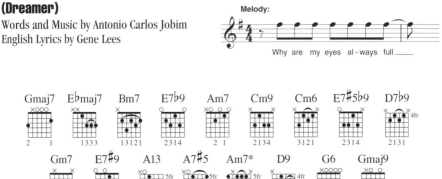

Melody:

Why are my eyes al - ways full ____

Verse 1

Gmaj7   **E♭maj7**
Why are my eyes always full of this vision of you?

Gmaj7
Why do I dream silly dreams

                                    Bm7 E7♭9
That I fear it won't come true?

Am7   **Cm9 Cm6**
I long to show you the stars

Bm7   **E7#5♭9**
Caught in the dark of the sea.

Am7   **D7♭9**
I long to speak of my love

                              Gmaj7 Gm7
But you won't come ___ to me.

	Gmaj7 **E♭maj7**
Verse 2	So I go on asking you, maybe someday you'll care.
	Gmaj7 **Bm7 E7♭9**
	I tell my sad little dreams to the soft evening air.
	Am7 **Cm9 Cm6**
	I am quite hopeless it seems,
	Bm7 **E7♯5♭9**
	Two things I know how to do,
	E7♯9 A13 A7♯5
	One is to dream,
	Am7* D9 G6 E♭maj7 Gmaj9
	Two is loving you.

Translated Lyrics

Verse Vivo sonhando, Sonhando mil horas sem fim
Tempo em que vou perguntando se gostas de mim
Tempo de falar em estrelas
Falar de um mar de um céu assin
Falar do bem que se tem mas você não vem
Não vem você não vindo, não vindo a vida tem fim
Gente que passa sorrindo zombando de mim
E eu a falar em estrelas, mar, amor, luar
Pobre de mim que só sei te amar.

Watch What Happens

from THE UMBRELLAS OF CHERBOURG

Music by Michel Legrand
Original French Text by Jacques Demy
English Lyrics by Norman Gimbel

Melody:

Let some - one _____ start be - liev - ing in

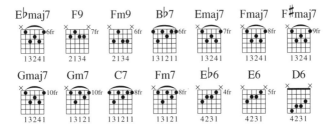

Ebmaj7   F9   Fm9   Bb7   Emaj7   Fmaj7   F#maj7

Gmaj7   Gm7   C7   Fm7   Eb6   E6   D6

Verse 1

    Ebmaj7   **F9**
Let someone start believing in you.

             Fm9
Let him hold out his hand.

Bb7   **Ebmaj7 Emaj7 Fmaj7 Emaj7**
 Let him touch you and watch   what   hap - pens.

Ebmaj7   **F9**
One someone who can look in your eyes

         Fm9
And see into your heart.

Bb7   **Ebmaj7 Emaj7 Fmaj7 Fmaj7**
 Let him find you and watch   what   hap - pens.

Bridge

    Gmaj7   **Gm7**   **C7**
Cold. No I won't believe your heart is cold.

     Fmaj7   **Fm7 B♭7**
Maybe just afraid to be broken a - gain.

Verse 2

    E♭maj7   **F9**
Let someone with a deep love to give,

         Fm9
Give that deep love to you

  B♭7   **E♭6**
 And what magic you'll see.

    E6 **D6**   **E♭6**
Let someone give his heart,

     E6 **D6**   **E♭6**
Some - one who cares like me.

Wave

Words and Music by
Antonio Carlos Jobim

So close your eyes, for that's a love-ly way

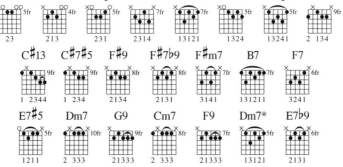

Intro ‖: Am9 D13 |Am9 D13 :‖

Verse 1

              Amaj7 F°7   **Em7**
So close your eyes, for that's a lovely way to be,

  A7♭9   **Dmaj7**   **Dm6**   **C♯13 C♯7♯5**
  Aware of things ___ your heart alone ___ was meant to see.

  F♯9   **F♯7♭9**   **F♯m7**   **B7**
  The funda - mental lone - liness goes

          F7   **E7♯5**   **Am9 D13**
Whenever two can dream a dream togeth - er.

Verse 2

  Am9 D13   **Amaj7 F°7**   **Em7**
      You can't de - ny, don't try to fight the rising sea.

  A7♭9   **Dmaj7**   **Dm6**
  Don't fight the moon, ___ the stars above,

          C♯13 C♯7♯5
And don't fight me.

F#9   F#7b9   F#m7   B7
The funda - mental lone - liness goes

        F7   E7#5   Am9 D13 Am9 D13
Whenever two can dream a dream togeth - er.

Bridge

    Dm7   G9   Em7
When I saw you first, the time was half past three.

    Cm7   F9   Dm7*
When your eyes met mine, it was e - ternity.

Verse 3

    E7b9   Amaj7 F°7   Em7
By now we know the wave is on its way to be.

    A7b9   Dmaj7   Dm6   C#13 C#7#5
Just catch the wave, ___ don't be afraid ___ of loving me.

    F#9   F#7b9   F#m7   B7
The funda - mental lone - liness goes

        F7   E7#5   Am9 D13 Am9 D13 Amaj7
Whenever two can dream a dream togeth - er.

Translated Lyrics

Verse 1   Vou te contar, os olhos já não podem ver,
Coisas que só coração pode entender.
Fundamental é mesmo o amor,
É impossível ser feliz sozinho.

Verse 2   O resto é mar, é tudo que não sei contar.
São coisas lindas, que eu tenho pr ate dar.
Vem de mansinho abrisa e mediz,
É impossível ser feliz sozinho.

Bridge   Da primeira vez era a cidade,
Da segunda o cais e a eternidade.

Verse 3   Agora eu já sei, da onda que se ergueu no mar,
E das estrelas que esquecemos de contar.
O amor se deixa surpreender,
Enquanto a noite vem nos envolver.

What a Diff'rence a Day Made

English Words by Stanley Adams
Music and Spanish Words by Maria Grever

Melody:

What a diff-'rence a day made,

Gm7   C7   Fmaj7   Bb9   Am7   A°7   Em7   A7

Dm7   G7   C7sus4   F9   Cm7   Bbmaj7   Eb9   F6

Verse 1

N.C.   Gm7
What a diff'rence a day made,

C7   Fmaj7 Bb9
  Twenty four little ho - urs,

Am7   Ab°7   Gm7
  Brought the sun and the flowers,

C7   Fmaj7
  Where there used to be rain.

                Em7
My yesterday was blue, dear,

A7   Dm7
  Today I'm part of you, dear.

              G7
My lonely nights are through, dear,

                         C7sus4
Since you said you were mine.

	C7	Gm7
Verse 2	What a diff'rence a day makes,	

C7   Fmaj7 B♭9
There's a rainbow be - fore   me,

Am7   A♭°7   Gm7
Skies a - bove can't be stormy

C7   F9   Cm7
Since that moment of bliss, that thrilling kiss.

F9   B♭maj7 E♭9   Fmaj7
It's heaven when you ___ find romance on your menu.

A♭°7   Gm7   C7   F6
What a difference a day made,   and the diff'rence is you.

Translated Lyrics

Verse 1

Cuando vuelva a tu lado,
No me niegues tus besos,
Que el amor que te he dado,
No podrás olvidar.
No me preguntes nada,
Que nada he de expli carte,
Que el beso que negaste,
Ya no lo puedes dár.

Verse 2

Cuando vuelva a tu lado,
Y es té sola contigo,
Las cosas que te digo,
No repitas jamás, por compasión,
Une tu labiio al mio,
Y estrechame en tus brazos.
Y cuenta los latidos,
De nuestro corazón.

What Now My Love

(Original French Title: "Et Maintenant")
Original French Lyric by Pierre Delano
Music by Francois Becaud
English Adaptation by Carl Sigman

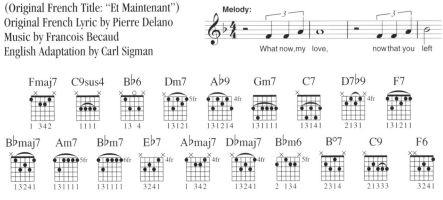

Verse 1

Fmaj7 C9sus4
What now, my love,

Fmaj7 C9sus4   B♭6 Fmaj7
  Now that you left   me?

Dm7 A♭9   Gm7 C7   Fmaj7 D7♭9
  How can I live _____ through another day

Gm7 C9sus4   Fmaj7 C9sus4
  Watching my dreams

Fmaj7 C9sus4   B♭6   Fmaj7
  Turning to ash - es

Dm7 A♭9   Gm7   C7   Fmaj7
  And my hopes ___ into bits of clay?

Bridge 1

F7   B♭maj7 Gm7   C7   Am7
  Once I could see,   once I could feel,

Dm7   Gm7   C7   Fmaj7
  Now I am numb, I've be - come un - real.

F7   B♭m7 E♭7   A♭maj7
I walk the night   without a goal

D♭maj7   B♭m6 B°7 C9sus4
  Stripped of my heart,   my   soul.

Verse 2

C9 C9sus4   Fmaj7 C9sus4
     What now, my love,

Fmaj7 C9sus4   B♭6 Fmaj7
     Now that it's o - ver.

Dm7 A♭9   Gm7 C7   Fmaj7 D7♭9
     I feel the world ____ closing in on me.

Gm7 C9sus4   Fmaj7 C9sus4
     Here come the stars

Fmaj7 C9sus4   B♭6   Fmaj7
     Tumbling a - round me.

Dm7 A♭9   Gm7 C7   Fmaj7
     There's the sky ____ where the sea should be.

Bridge 2

F7   B♭maj7 Gm7 C7   Am7
     What now, my love,   now that you're gone.

Dm7   Gmajm7   C7   Fmaj7
     I'd be a fool to go on and on.

   F7   B♭m7 E♭7   A♭maj7
No one would care,   no one would cry

D♭maj7   B♭m6   B°7 C9sus4
     If I should live   or   die.

Outro

C9 C9sus4   Fmaj7 C9sus4
     What now, my love,

Fmaj7 C9sus4   B♭6   Fmaj7
     Now there is noth - ing.

Dm7 A♭9   Gm7 C7   Fmaj7 F6
     Only my last ____ good - bye.

You Belong to My Heart

(Solamente Una Vez)

Music and Spanish Words by Agustin Lara
English Words by Ray Gilbert

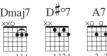

Dmaj7	D#°7	A7	Em7	D	D6

Verse 1

    Dmaj7 **D#°7** **A7**
You belong to my heart now and for - ever

      Em7 **A7** **Dmaj7**
And our love had its start not long a - go.

Em7 A7   **D**
  We were gathering stars

      D#°7   **A7**
While a million gui - tars played our love song,

   Em7   **A7**   **Dmaj7**
When I said, "I love you," ev'ry beat of my heart said it too.

Verse 2

  Em7 **A7** **Dmaj7**
'Twas a moment like this,

  D#°7 **A7**
Do you re - member?

      Em7 **A7** **Dmaj7**
And your eyes threw a kiss when they met mine.

Em7 A7   **D**   **D#°7**   **A7**
  Now we own all the stars and a million gui - tars are still playing.

   Em7   **A7**   **D6**
Darling, you are the song and you'll always belong to my heart.

Translated Lyrics

Verse 1   Solamente una vez amé en la vida,
Solamente una vez y nada más.
Una vez nada más en mi huerto brilló la esperanza,
La esperanza que alumbra el camino de mi soledad.

Verse 2   Una vez nada más se entre ga el alma,
Con la dulce y total renunciación
Y cuando ese milagro realize el prodigio de amarse,
Hay campanas de fiesta que cantan en el corazón.

Zingaro
(Retrato em Branco e Preto)
Words by Chico Buarque de Hollanda
Music by Antonio Carlos Jobim

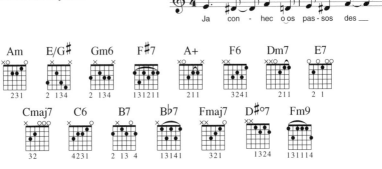

Verse 1

   Am   **E/G#**
Já conheç o os passos des estra - da.

       Gm6
Sei que não vai dar em na ___ da.

  F#7   **A+ F6**
Seus seg - redos sei de cor.

Dm7   **E7**   **Cmaj7**
Sá conheç o as pedras do caminho.

    C6   **B7**
E sei tam - bém que ali soz in - ho.

      E7
Eu vou ficar tanto pior.

   Bb7   **Am**
O que é posso contra o encan - to.

       E/G#
Desse a mor que eu nego tan - to.

      Gm6
Evï to tanto. E que no en tan - to.

  F#7   **Fmaj7**
Volta sempre a enfeiticar.

Dm7	D#°7	Am

Com seus mesmos tristes velhos fa - tos.

Fmaj7   **Dm7**

Que num álbum de retra ___ tos.

Fm9   **E7** **Am**

Eu tei - mo em cul - ecionar.

Verse 2

Am   **E/G#**

Lá voy eu, de nova como um to - lo.

               Gm6

Procurar a descon so - lo.

    F#7   **A+ F6**

Que can - sel de conhecer.

Dm7   **E7**   **Cmaj7**

Novos dias tristes, noites cla - ras.

    C6   **B7**

Versos cartas, minha ca - ra.

              E7

Ainda volto a ihe escrever.

      Bb7   **Am**

Pra lhe diz - er que isso é peca - do.

               E/G#

Eu trago o peito tao mar ca - do.

               Gm6

De lambranças do passa - do.

    F#7   **Fmaj7**

E vo - cê sabe a cazão.

Dm7   **D#°7**

Vou colecio nar mais um

   Am   **Fmaj7**

Sonet - o outro re trato em branco

   Dm7   **Fm9** **E7** **Am**

E pre - to a maltra - tar meu coracão.

Yours

(Cuando Se Quiere de Veras)

Words by Albert Gamse and Jack Sherr
Music by Gonzalo Roig

Melody:

Yours   till ____   the   stars   lose __   their

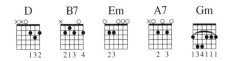

D	B7	Em	A7	Gm
1 3 2	2 1 3 4	2 3	2 3	1 3 4 1 1 1

Verse

    D
Yours till the stars lose their glory.

                B7 Em
Yours till the birds fail to   sing.

               A7
Yours to the end of life's story,

               D
This pledge to you, dear, I bring.

Yours in the gray of December,

B7   **Em**
Here or on far distant shores.

            A7   **D7**   **B7 Em**
I've never loved an - y - one the way I love you.

B7   **Em**
How could I

     Gm D   **A7 D**
When I was born to be just yours?

Guitar Chord Songbooks

Each book includes complete lyrics, chord symbols, and guitar chord diagrams.

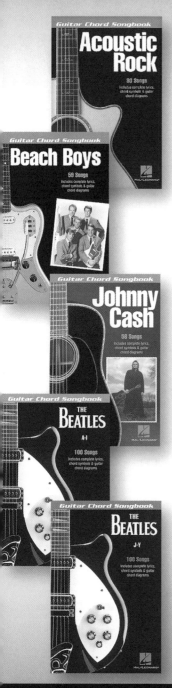

Acoustic Rock
80 acoustic favorites: Blackbird • Blowin' in the Wind • Layla • Maggie May • Me and Julio down by the Schoolyard • Pink Houses • and more.
00699540.. $17.95

Alabama
50 of Alabama's best: Born Country • Dixieland Delight • Feels So Right • Mountain Music • Song of the South • Why Lady Why • and more.
00699914 .... $14.95

The Beach Boys
59 favorites: California Girls • Don't Worry Baby • Fun, Fun, Fun • Good Vibrations • Help Me Rhonda • Wouldn't It Be Nice • dozens more!
00699566.. $14.95

Blues
80 blues tunes: Big Boss Man • Cross Road Blues (Crossroads) • Damn Right, I've Got the Blues • Pride and Joy • Route 66 • Sweet Home Chicago • and more.
00699733 .... $12.95

Broadway
80 stage hits: All I Ask of You • Bali Ha'i • Edelweiss • Hello, Dolly! • Memory • Ol' Man River • People • Seasons of Love • Sunrise, Sunset • and more.
00699920 .... $14.99

Johnny Cash
58 Cash classics: A Boy Named Sue • Cry, Cry, Cry • Daddy Sang Bass • Folsom Prison Blues • I Walk the Line • RIng of Fire • Solitary Man • and more.
00699648.. $16.95

The Beatles (A-I)
An awesome reference of Beatles hits: All You Need Is Love • The Ballad of John and Yoko • Get Back • Good Day Sunshine • A Hard Day's Night • Hey Jude • I Saw Her Standing There • and more!
00699558.. $17.99

The Beatles (J-Y)
100 more Beatles hits: Lady Madonna • Let It Be • Ob-La-Di, Ob-La-Da • Paperback Writer • Revolution • Twist and Shout • When I'm Sixty-Four • and more.
00699562.. $17.99

Steven Curtis Chapman
65 from this CCM superstar: Be Still and Know • Cinderella • For the Sake of the Call • Live Out Loud • Speechless • With Hope • and more.
00700702 .... $14.99

Children's Songs
70 songs for kids: Alphabet Song • Bingo • The Candy Man • Eensy Weensy Spider • Puff the Magic Dragon • Twinkle, Twinkle Little Star • and more!
00699539.. $14.95

Complete contents listings available online at www.halleonard.com

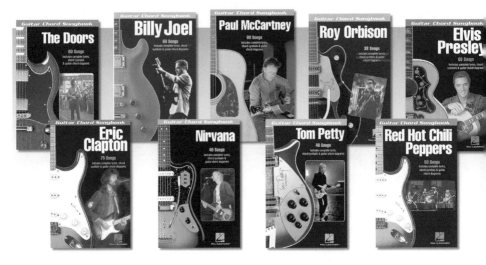

Christmas Carols

80 Christmas carols: Angels We Have Heard on High • The Holly and the Ivy • I Saw Three Ships • Joy to the World • O Holy Night • Silent Night • What Child Is This? • and more.
00699536...$12.95

Christmas Songs

80 Christmas favorites: The Christmas Song • Feliz Navidad • Jingle-Bell Rock • Merry Christmas, Darling • Rudolph the Red-Nosed Reindeer • more.
00699537...$12.95

Eric Clapton

75 of Slowhand's finest: I Shot the Sheriff • Knockin' on Heaven's Door • Layla • Strange Brew • Tears in Heaven • Wonderful Tonight • and more!
00699567...$15.99

Classic Rock

80 rock essentials: Beast of Burden • Cat Scratch Fever • Hot Blooded • Money • Rhiannon • Sweet Emotion • Walk on the Wild Side • more
00699598...$15.99

Contemporary Christian

80 hits from today's top CCM artists: Awesome God • El Shaddai • Friends • His Strength Is Perfect • I Will Be Here • A Maze of Grace • Run to You • more.
00699564...$14.95

Country

80 country standards: Boot Scootin' Boogie • Crazy • Hey, Good Lookin'• Sixteen Tons • Through the Years • Your Cheatin' Heart • more.
00699534...$14.95

Country Favorites

Over 60 songs: Achy Breaky Heart (Don't Tell My Heart) • Brand New Man • Gone Country • The Long Black Veil • Make the World Go Away • and more.
00700609 ....$14.99

Country Standards

60 songs: By the Time I Get to Phoenix • El Paso • The Gambler • I Fall to Pieces • Jolene • King of the Road • Put Your Hand in the Hand • A Rainy Night in Georgia • more.
00700608 ....$12.95

Cowboy Songs

Over 60 tunes: Back in the Saddle Again • Happy Trails • Home on the Range • Streets of Laredo • The Yellow Rose of Texas • and more.
00699636...$12.95

The Doors

60 classics: Break on Through to the Other Side • The End • L.A. Woman • Light My Fire • Love Her Madly • Love Me Two Times • People Are Strange • Riders on the Storm • Twentieth Century Fox • and more.
00699888 ....$15.99

Early Rock

80 early rock classics: All I Have to Do Is Dream • Fever • He's So Fine • I'm Sorry • Lollipop • Puppy Love • Sh-Boom (Life Could Be a Dream) • and more.
00699916 ....$14.99

Folk Pop Rock

80 songs: American Pie • Dust in the Wind • Me and Bobby McGee • Somebody to Love • Time in a Bottle • and more.
00699651...$14.95

Folksongs

80 folk favorites: Aura Lee • Camptown Races • Danny Boy • Man of Constant Sorrow • Nobody Knows the Trouble I've Seen • When the Saints Go Marching In • and more.
00699541...$12.95

Gospel Hymns

80 hymns: Amazing Grace • Give Me That Old Time Religion • I Love to Tell the Story • The Old Rugged Cross • Shall We Gather at the River? • Wondrous Love • and more.
00700463 ....$14.99

Grand Ole Opry®
80 great songs: Abilene • Act Naturally • Country Boy • Crazy • Friends in Low Places • He Stopped Loving Her Today • Wings of a Dove • dozens more!
00699885 ....$16.95

Hillsong United
65 top worship songs: Break Free • Everyday • From the Inside Out • God Is Great • Look to You • Now That You're Near • Salvation Is Here • To the Ends of the Earth • and more.
00700222 ....$12.95

Jazz Standards
50 songs: Ain't Misbehavin' • Cheek to Cheek • In the Wee Small Hours of the Morning • The Nearness of You • Stardust • The Way You Look Tonight • and more.
00700972 ....$14.95

Billy Joel
60 Billy Joel favorites: • It's Still Rock and Roll to Me • The Longest Time • Piano Man • She's Always a Woman • Uptown Girl • We Didn't Start the Fire • You May Be Right • and more.
00699632..$15.99

Elton John
60 songs: Bennie and the Jets • Candle in the Wind • Crocodile Rock • Goodbye Yellow Brick Road • Pinball Wizard • Sad Songs (Say So Much) • Tiny Dancer • Your Song • and more.
00699732 ....$15.99

Latin
50 favorites: Bésame Mucho (Kiss Me Much) • The Girl from Ipanema (Garôta De Ipanema) • The Look of Love • So Nice (Summer Samba) • and more.
00700973 ....$14.95

Paul McCartney
60 from Sir Paul: Band on the Run • Jet • Let 'Em In • Maybe I'm Amazed • No More Lonely Nights • Say Say Say • Take It Away • With a Little Luck • more!
00385035 ....$16.95

Motown
50 Motown masterpieces: ABC • Baby I Need Your Lovin' • I'll Be There • Just My Imagination • Lady Marmalade • Stop! In the Name of Love • You Can't Hurry Love • more.
00699734 ....$16.95

The 1950s
80 early rock favorites: High Hopes • Mister Sandman • Only You (And You Alone) • Put Your Head on My Shoulder • Que Sera, Sera (Whatever Will Be, Will Be) • Tammy • That's Amoré • and more.
00699922 ....$14.99

The 1980s
80 hits: Centerfold • Come on Eileen • Don't Worry, Be Happy • Got My Mind Set on You • Sailing • Should I Stay or Should I Go • Sweet Dreams (Are Made of This) • more.
00700551 ....$16.99

Nirvana
40 songs: About a Girl • Come as You Are • Heart Shaped Box • The Man Who Sold the World • Smells like Teen Spirit • You Know You're Right • and more.
00699762 ....$16.99

Roy Orbison
38 songs: Blue Bayou • Crying • Oh, Pretty Woman • Only the Lonely (Know the Way I Feel) • Pretty Paper • Running Scared • Working for the Man • You Got It • and more.
00699752 ....$12.95

Tom Petty
American Girl • Breakdown • Don't Do Me like That • Free Fallin' • Here Comes My Girl • Into the Great Wide Open • Mary Jane's Last Dance • Refugee • Runnin' Down a Dream • The Waiting • more.
00699883 ....$15.99

Pop/Rock
80 chart hits: Against All Odds • Come Sail Away • Every Breath You Take • Hurts So Good • Kokomo • More Than Words • Smooth • Summer of '69 • and more.
00699538..$14.95

Praise and Worship
80 favorites: Agnus Dei • He Is Exalted • I Could Sing of Your Love Forever • Lord, I Lift Your Name on High • More Precious Than Silver • Open the Eyes of My Heart • Shine, Jesus, Shine • and more.
00699634 ....$12.95

Elvis Presley
60 hits: All Shook Up • Blue Suede Shoes • Can't Help Falling in Love • Heartbreak Hotel • Hound Dog • Jailhouse Rock • Suspicious Minds • Viva Las Vegas • more.
00699633..$14.95

Red Hot Chili Peppers
50 hits: Breaking the Girl • By the Way • Californication • Give It Away • Higher Ground • Love Rollercoaster • Scar Tissue • Suck My Kiss • Under the Bridge • What It Is • and more.
00699710..$16.95

Rock 'n' Roll
80 rock 'n' roll classics: At the Hop • Great Balls of Fire • It's My Party • La Bamba • My Boyfriend's Back • Peggy Sue • Stand by Me • more.
00699535..$14.95

Sting
50 favorites from Sting and the Police: Brand New Day • Can't Stand Losing You • Don't Stand So Close to Me • Every Breath You Take • Fields of Gold • King of Pain • Message in a Bottle • Roxanne • more.
00699921 ....$14.99

Three Chord Songs
65 includes: All Right Now • La Bamba • Lay Down Sally • Mony, Mony • Rock Around the Clock • Rock This Town • Werewolves of London • You Are My Sunshine • and more.
00699720 ....$12.95